Behavior in Small Groups

Alfred Benjamin
University of Haifa, Israel

Houghton Mifflin Company   Boston

Dallas   Geneva, Illinois   Hopewell, New Jersey
Palo Alto   London

Printed in the U.S.A.
Library of Congress Catalog Card Number: 77-073213
ISBN: 0-395-25447-7

To my parents
Jane and Paul Benjamin

Contents

Preface

It has been my privilege and pleasure to work with groups and to train students who wish to lead groups for the past twenty or so years, and I remain convinced that group work is important and should be a pleasurable experience for both members and leaders. Members come to groups in order to grow and to learn to enlarge their horizons — cognitive, emotional, and behavioral. The leader's role is to facilitate these learnings. I am convinced that the skills needed to lead groups successfully are acquired through much experience and accompanying supervision and that no adequate substitute exists for these. However, books can assist the neophyte in group work to think, to plan, and to synthesize what has been learned.

Since I am not aware of the existence of the sort of book I have often wished to recommend to beginners in this field, I have decided to write one. There is, of course, a vast literature in the area of work with groups. That I have been influenced by much of it will become apparent from this text. Yet what the beginner needs right at hand is a book dealing with the very problems he or she is confronting. It is my hope that in the following pages the beginner will find food for thought and be stimulated to discern solutions that all potential group leaders must ultimately find for themselves.

Group work is both a technique and an art. The former can be learned and polished with time. The latter is intuitive, but it can be acquired — to some extent at least — with experience, reflection, personal growth, and maturity. I shall attempt to deal primarily with the technique because I do not know whether it is possible to write about the art. It is my hope that you, the reader, will be able to concentrate on the art of group work and on your style, once you no longer need to concern yourself predominantly with technique.

Group work is one area on which a professional person can concentrate when trying to help others. Involvement in group work is not a profession in its own right, but of necessity it demands professional content and focus. Counseling, psychotherapy, social work, guidance, and other professional skills can be and are being used with groups as well as with individual clients. Therefore, the individual who wishes to lead groups must first become proficient in a given helping profession and then learn the technique of group work.

At the outset, the helping professions assumed the characteristics of a dyadic relationship: a physician, expert, or helper who matched with a patient, client, or helpee. Making the transition from one client to eight, ten, or fifteen while holding the number of experts at one (with the addition of an observer and/or coexpert at times) constituted not merely a quantitative but a qualitative change. The dyad has evolved into a group; what was appropriate for the former is not necessarily appropriate for the latter, for the needs of the group are often very different from those of the encounter of two people.

For at least a generation, group work has been very popular in many of the helping professions, with both clients and professionals. Although the specific reasons for this development do not concern us here, it is clear that groups are much in demand. Naturally enough, they are both criticized and praised, attacked and defended. For the foreseeable future, however, they are here to stay. There is something about them that attracts member and leader alike: they constitute a miniature society, they enable us to learn together and from one another, they promise personal interactions and a sense of belonging. They offer, at least potentially, basic human warmth and understanding.

This book is not about sensitivity training, but it has been greatly influenced by the theory and practice of that particular area of group work. I have taught courses in group processes for a number of years and have led many human relations workshops. As a matter of fact, I finally decided to write this book after a very specific experience in this field, an experience that forced me to reflect on the benefits and limitations of sensitivity training as a training tool for potential leaders of groups other than T-Groups. I do feel certain that a professionally conducted T-Group has much to offer the neophyte group leader in terms of personal growth. It may also teach the group leader techniques for helping members to communicate better with themselves and with others. However, the inherent lack of structure as well as initial frustrations and ambiguities that are essential and legitimate in the T-Group will confuse and mislead the newcomer when he or she tries to transfer these qualities to other groups, either because the newcomer assumes that this is how the group should be or because he or she has not learned any alternative ways of functioning. It is partly to eliminate this confusion and to suggest clear alternatives that I am writing this book.

In the pages that follow I intend to discuss the dynamics of group life, examine the fears, anxieties, and doubts of beginners in group work, look at various aspects of the makeup and functioning of groups, ponder the skills required by group members and group leaders, and assess the varied procedures in use today for training group leaders. In brief, I wish to share my perceptions of what goes on in groups with you who are just entering the field, with the hope that these perceptions will help clarify and broaden your own perceptions. Once at home in the technique of group work, you will be able to develop the art and your own style.

I, myself, have been influenced by much that I have read, but even more by the many exciting experiences I have lived through in groups. To all those who have allowed me to share their experiencing, theorizing, thinking, and feeling, I am deeply grateful. They are too numerous to mention, but I hope that many will recognize their contributions to my present frame of reference. As always, my wife Aliza (Joyce) has proven a critical, patient, and most helpful editor. I wish to thank my publishers, Houghton Mifflin, for their understanding and indulgence of some of my idiosyncrasies.

A. B.

Behavior in Small Groups

1

The Dynamics of Small Groups: An Overview

PRELUDE: ASHKELON

Ashkelon is a small town on the Mediterranean coast, a few miles south of Tel Aviv, somnolent in winter and teaming with tourists in summer. As I approached this seaside resort early one morning in early July of 1975 to attend a three-day meeting of the Israel Psychological Association, at which I had agreed to lead one of the proffered workshops, I was quite annoyed with myself for having consented to come. Nothing much could possibly be accomplished in a three-day sensitivity training workshop, even though participation was entirely voluntary and everyone had been told that sea and pool were to be enjoyed only during the early afternoon breaks. But what — if people decided to swim, sunbathe, and relax rather than worry about their personal growth and impact on others — could or should be done? I, for one, would not blame them; I could only blame myself for having agreed to come.

As it turned out, my fears proved unfounded. Hundreds of members of the Association streamed into the local hotels, and more than twenty workshops were quickly organized. I enjoyed mine very much. I found members genuinely caring about their effect on others and interested in learning more about themselves. We experienced frustration and confusion, fight and flight, love and hate. We joked and were serious. We swam as well and got in a bit of sunbathing, but the group had come to work and work it did.

As our time together drew to a close, members asked for a last session in which to sum up what we had accomplished and to examine their learnings. In that final session, one central theme soon predominated: the transfer of learnings to the back-home situation where participants all led or wished to lead groups — not sensitivity training but counseling, therapy, or guidance groups.

Are the frustrations and ambiguities that we had at first encountered desirable in those back-home situations? How much structure should leaders provide in their groups? Should they be as passive as I had been at the beginning? Under what conditions do people learn best in groups? How should members be selected? How should groups be composed? How often should they meet? Isn't the dyadic — one-to-one — relationship really preferable? As we tried to cope with these and other questions, I became dimly aware of an uneasy feeling that gradually came to the fore during the long ride back to Haifa.

I had been asked serious questions by professionally trained psychologists. These were not posed defensively during the course of the workshop, designed perhaps to avoid deeper interpersonal communication. They surfaced at the end, during the summing up, and reflected real concern. I recalled other situations where similar topics had arisen for discussion. Perhaps I had never dealt with them satisfactorily? If experienced professionals are perplexed, how must neophyte professionals feel? And so, slowly but surely, the present book began to crystallize in my mind.

Then came the doubts. There exists a vast and excellent literature in the area of groups. Is it not presumptuous on my part to think that one more slim volume will really make a difference? Furthermore, are there answers, and, if so, do I possess at least some of them? Assuming that I do, will they assist the insecure and perplexed neophyte? One day, some months later, I knew just what I had to do: write a book addressed primarily to those professionals who are competent and confident in their own fields of specialization, but uncertain and inexperienced in group work, which they now wish to undertake. My contribution would consist of a personal account of the answers I have found for myself and the questions that remain unanswered. It is my hope that what I have learned from others and from myself will provide beginners with a frame of reference while they continue to seek those answers that will, in the long run, prove most meaningful to them.

SENSITIVITY TRAINING
AND THE GROUP LEADER

It is my contention that sensitivity training, which is widely used today to teach professionals and non-professionals alike, can if properly and ethically carried out provide new group leaders with many important insights (Lakin, 1972). However, leaders must be discriminating in culling those learnings they can transfer with benefit to their own groups. They must separate these from newly gained insights they consider to be their own learnings, and try not to impose personal learnings on the groups they are to lead. Group goals are not identical to those of sensitivity training.

Sensitivity training is a form of experiential learning within a small group of approximately twelve members. Their meetings may be concentrated intensively or staggered over a relatively long period of time. Participants engage in learning about their own behavior and its impact upon others. Sensitivity training stresses the here and now — what is actually occurring in the group while it meets — and takes place in a permissive atmosphere where such learning is encouraged by a leader or trainer who provides minimal structure, no specific agenda, and few defined norms. The emphasis is on learning how to learn, and the vacuum ensuing from the leader's refusal to "lead" is deliberately created to forward this aim. In the main, the leader analyzes and encourages others to analyze group and individual experience. The major goals of sensitivity training are to promote self-insight and change, and the understanding of effective group process and interpersonal dynamics, as well as to foster the development of skills for diagnosing individual, group, and organizational behavior.

The T-Group (Bradford et al., 1965), a term used synonymously with sensitivity training, may well provide you with many new and significant learnings — that is, if you are highly motivated, more or less "normal," not too dependent a personality, and not pressed too hard by the leader (Lieberman et al., 1973). You may begin to see yourself in a different light, more in line with the way others perceive you. You may assess your strengths and weaknesses anew, as the result of having mutually examined these with others. Encouraged by feedback from the group, you may attempt unfamiliar behaviors to see how they feel and to determine whether they fit. Some of these behaviors you may go on trying while others you will reject. You may share some of your fears, hopes, and anxieties and come away richer for the experience. You may feel the warmth that comes from being an integral part of a group; you may help others and be helped in turn. You may learn to listen better and to become more responsive to nonverbal cues. You may learn once again, but this time on a deeper level, that people are really different from each other — they do not always perceive or think or feel or react as you do. You may begin to acquire new skills in interpersonal communication. You may become more sensitive to the needs of others and to your own as well. You may feel group pressure: succumb to it, resist it, respond to it as openly as you know how. You may mull over what makes groups tick. You may . . . the list of possible learnings is long.

Much of this you will, of course, legitimately transfer to the groups you will yourself be leading. But there is a caveat and it is crucial. Your T-Group leaders, undoubtedly, are quite passive during the early phase of group development. They most probably provide minimal structure: they offer no agenda, and do not decide what to discuss or how to discuss it. They barely set norms, but allow you to flounder and fret. They sit there, cool, calm, and collected while you become more and more frustrated, angry, and upset by the ambiguous situation. It is precisely this lack of structure and leadership that you dare not transfer into your own groups.

Let us assume that you are a school counselor, whose clients come for group counseling. They arrive more or less motivated, generally of their own free choice, presumably knowing what they are getting into, and, ostensibly, willing to give the group and you a chance. They will need and expect — and will have every right to expect — that you will structure the setting for them, and that you will be as active as necessary for that particular group to achieve its learning goals. You will wish to help them move toward these goals, and will have to guide and influence them in that direction from the very beginning.

I am not considering, for the moment, the style of leadership you adopt: group-centered, laissez faire, authoritarian, or democratic. I am suggesting that the very structure and positive leadership you did *not* receive at the onset of your T-Group, you must provide at the onset of the groups you lead. How, specifically, you will behave in this and other situations will depend on many factors, some of which we shall look into as we proceed. Providing structure and active leadership as your group begins to function does not in itself imply that you are an authoritarian leader. As a matter of fact, the typical trainer behavior in sensitivity training, at the outset at least, is far from democratic. It is precisely because people tend to need structure and leadership that they become so terribly frustrated and confused when they realize that the T-Group leader will not provide them. This teaching without structure or leadership is often very effective, indeed; however, it is not what members would choose were they asked. In that sense sensitivity training facilitators are extremely authoritarian. Their clients can generally take it and they stay. Yours cannot, and may well run away.

Chances are that the members of your group have never before participated in a learning experience of the type you are providing. It will take time, patience, and occasional prodding to discover how ready and motivated they are. Meanwhile, they will want to know what is expected of them, what they may expect of you, what the goals of the group are, and how they are to be achieved. In short, they are naive and inexperienced in the ways of group life and will look to you for direction. Something in their lives is upsetting them and preventing them from functioning adequately. They have agreed to come because they need help. They do not know as yet that they may be able to help one another; right now they are expecting your guidance and leadership. They are entitled to both. How you structure the situation, the ultimate climate that will prevail, and the communication network that will develop in the group are, to a great extent, a function of your leadership style. The point is that you must lead.

A psychologist leading a newly formed group of parents in a child guidance clinic might open in this manner:

> As you may remember, my name is ———. I've met with each of you individually to discuss your participation in the group. I'm glad you all decided to come. We'll be meeting every Tuesday morning from nine to ten-thirty. The purpose of the group is for us to help one another in our relations with our children. I shall try to do my share, but I feel certain that there is a great deal we all have in common, and that, as a group, we can learn a lot from one another. Perhaps someone is willing to introduce him- or herself. After the introductions, we can decide what to talk about first. . . .

Meanwhile, in this as in any other new group, members are looking around. They are probably wondering why others have come, what their problems are, whom they will like, whether the group can really help. And in this there lies another important lesson for the beginning group leader: members are looking not only at you; they are concerned not only with you and your behavior. They are already beginning to feel each other out, to size each other up. They are starting to interact. They have much more in common, one with the other, than they have with you, and they are drawing together. They need you now to get things going, to help matters along, but they are already becoming involved in the group, not sure of what it can do for them and yet hoping that it will prove worthwhile.

THE DYNAMICS OF GROUP LIFE

Every group develops its own unique character, and yet all groups present to the observer certain common features that enable us to speak of the dynamics of groups. I wish to point out some of these, because frequently new leaders tend to overlook these common features, being primarily concerned, naturally enough, with their own role and behavior. The truth of the matter is that because of leaders, despite them, or not directly related to them, certain forces come into play within the group, certain aspects of group life emerge over which leaders have little control but whose development they must observe carefully and nurture sensitively.

Group leaders have much in common with orchestra leaders. Whether the rhythm is fast or slow, tempestuous or calm, their batons will be wielded. Unless the orchestra has learned over considerable time to work together smoothly, pandemonium is likely to break loose in the orchestra leader's absence. Although the musicians will not constantly look at the conductor or require continual signals, he or she must be there when needed, and must know when to give proper cues and essential direction.

Group leaders must at all times be alert to the dynamics of their groups and ready to intervene if it is necessary to exert influence. They are certainly not constantly active and may often appear to be not active enough; they may, indeed, seem oblivious at times to what is going on in their groups, but they must be trusted to act, to interfere, to contribute when needed — and they can earn this trust only if they behave accordingly.

As a new leader you will soon become aware of some of the unique characteristics of group life. Sharing in it from your own vantage point, you will learn to recognize these characteristics, and to decide when, if, and how to make your contributions. I will refer to the characteristics of group life throughout the book; here I wish merely to introduce some of the major features of the dynamics of groups.

1. *Group reality.* The group will define its reality for itself. Consciously or unconsciously, by consensus, vote, or imposition, it will define what is real for it and how to deal with that reality.

2. *Group norms.* Slowly but surely, the group will set its own norms of behavior and will enforce these on its members, at times democratically, at others tyrannically. Members will not always be able to define these standards explicitly, but they will usually brook no violation of them.

3. *Membership.* In most cases, although the group itself does not choose its members, it exercises strong influence on them from the outset. The group, rather early in its life, will cast members in specific roles from which they may find it difficult or even impossible to deviate. It will, in addition, control the interactions of its members and provide them with good, fair, or poor reality testing.

4. *Group leadership.* From within the group itself an informal leadership will emerge, consisting of one or several participants. This leadership will encourage or discourage member involvement, form coalitions and factions, or attempt to rule unilaterally. It will cooperate with, oppose, or act independently of the formal group leader.

5. *Group climate.* Finally, the group will offer members a climate in which to learn. This climate may be warm or cold, friendly, hostile, or simply neutral. The atmosphere ultimately prevailing in the group will influence the members' sense of belonging. As a consequence, they will come to meetings either gladly or reluctantly, or may even eventually drop out.

Obviously, in all of the above-mentioned areas there is much for the leader to notice and to contribute. The leader must carefully observe what is taking place in the group, and be prepared to express impressions of group activity at appropriate moments. At other times the leader must empathize aloud with individual members, in order to show them and the group a sensitivity to individual as well as to group needs and learnings. In short, the leader has to behave in a way that assists the entire group to move ahead in a constructive fashion.

DYADS AND GROUPS

What considerations should guide us when weighing with our clients the decision to work in a dyadic relationship or in a group? The question will not always arise, of course. For instance, there may be no prospective group in the offing or, alternatively, the client may not be able to afford individual help. At times the client may know exactly which he or she prefers, and you may agree that it is the best choice. Still, the problem will not always be so easily solved, and it is worth considering briefly now.

The goals are very similar. Both dyad and group offer potential clients an opportunity to understand themselves and their behaviors better, so that they may change in directions enabling them to lead richer, more satisfying lives, and to behave in ways that will improve their interactions with significant persons. But there do exist basic differences. This remains true even when we admit the fact that a dyad is a group, the smallest group possible.

In the **dyadic relationship** — counselor/client, therapist/patient, helper/helpee — the stress is likely to be placed on the **intrapersonal**, whereas in the group it tends to be on the **interpersonal**. Beyond learning from myself, in the dyad I can learn from the authority; in the group I may be able to learn from other group members as well. Group learnings tend to be less intensive, less focused on my own personal needs, perhaps less satisfying narcissistically, although it cannot be denied that some group members do extremely well in satisfying that particular need even in groups. The group is a microsociety possessing its own dynamics. It develops needs and satisfactions of its own that outweigh, at times, those of individual members. The group tends to emphasize *social*, while the dyad emphasizes *personal*, competence. It must not be overlooked, however, that when the group leader and a member interact in a helper/helpee relationship within the group, a dyadic situation has been created for the moment that may benefit not only that particular member but, vicariously, the entire group.

Beyond all this, we can accurately predict so very little — for example, how our client will react to the authority figure in the dyad or group, or how he or she may affect or be affected by the members of a group — that we do well to support the particular preferences of those we wish to help, when a choice can in fact be made. In the helping professions, luckily, the client's commitment need not be final.

As for you, the neophyte professional, I suggest you first become familiar with and secure in the dyadic relationship. Experience has taught me that this will make it easier for you to move on to group work, once you have acquired the additional skills needed. Incidentally when setting up a therapy group, it is important to check whether any of the candidates is already engaged in dyadic therapy, so that you can consult with the therapist as to whether group work in addition is contraindicated at present. To round out the picture, somewhat: it happens frequently that after a relatively intensive group experience, some members become interested in and feel ready for a dyadic relationship. The reverse also holds true. A meaningful dyadic relationship may encourage the client to seek a group experience.

HERE AND NOW; THERE AND THEN

Those who are involved simultaneously in a dyadic and a group experience will notice rather soon yet another important difference. While the distinction is by no means clear-cut or absolute, it is true, I believe, that the group works more on the here and now — what is presently taking place within the group — whereas in the dyad considerable time may be spent exploring "there and then" events: experiences, memories, happenings from somewhere in the past life of the client. Even the group cannot live on here and now material exclusively, but members can use it to good advantage. Since every member present is a part of the here and now, it is possible to check out how everyone perceives a given situation: what was said, what was heard, what was intended, what was hinted at, and so forth.

In addition, members may learn how they come across to others and just what in their behavior fosters the impressions created. This kind of feedback, which will be discussed more fully later on, can be used in the dyad as well, but in a much more restricted fashion since only the authority figure is involved in the interaction and no other checking out is possible for the moment. On the other hand, the total involvement facilitated by the dyad is very difficult to achieve and maintain for every group member at every stage of group development.

At this point I feel it necessary to discuss a specific type of group, one in whose work the there and then is of tremendous importance, where it must be kept in view even while here and now material is being discussed. I am referring to the group that constitutes a team that either works together closely or whose members tend to interact with one another from time to time at a given institution or enterprise. This is a group that meets as a team with a particular task as its goal — for instance, to improve communication and further interpersonal relations at work. The members of such a team are not strangers to each other. They share a past history, of which the group leader may be totally unaware, that is bound to affect their present actions and interactions. They often come into daily contact, and not just when the group meets, which may be once a week at best. Hopefully, they will not disperse when the group terminates, and their mutual impact on each other will undoubtedly outlast the lifetime of the group.

Under such circumstances the there and then can hardly be ignored. It will have to be woven carefully into the fabric of the present if the group's goal is to be achieved. Members of such a team are not responsible to themselves alone; they are accountable to a larger system, be it factory, school, hospital, or community. These members do not meet as strangers interested in discovering what hierarchy will develop in the group. They arrive already imbued with authority, power, status, or the lack thereof. Each one knows where he or she stands, and the others know it as well. The group will not easily recast its members in new roles, but will tend to relate to member roles as they are perceived on the outside. The group may not be able to deal with the present unless and until it delves into its common past. When status and power are at stake — and perhaps a job as well — members will not readily confront one another openly and candidly.

Here the leader must tread warily indeed. Issues pertaining to work may not be an escape from, but rather a confrontation of, interpersonal concerns. Intrapersonal concerns may not appear at all, as they may not seem appropriate in a framework set up to deal with interpersonal matters affecting work. When they are brought up, they may well be totally ignored or shunted aside as irrelevant. Of course, it will not always be easy to decide what is appropriate to the defined task; if the leader has strong doubts, these should be referred to the group.

Because of yet another factor, I have come to the conclusion that it is unwise to press too hard in this type of group, but essential to restrict members to what is relevant in the context of their specific task: helping them to adhere closely to the common goal of greater work efficiency and better interpersonal communication, which is eventually to be transferred to day-to-day interactions. The factor I am referring to is voluntary participation.

I never take for granted the voluntary participation of any member in any group. He or she may have been pressured into the group by instances unknown to me and, at times, not even entirely clear to the member. In group work with a team, the situation is still more complicated. I may not know who initiated the idea of working as a group with an outside consultant; who was in favor, who opposed; who dared show opposition openly, and who feigned consent. When one is a member of a team, it is difficult to tell others to go ahead and try to improve interpersonal communication while remaining aloof oneself. If one is a central member of the team, refusal to participate may jeopardize the entire undertaking. It is much simpler to play along. My experience with such teams has been that only when genuine personal commitment on the part of every — or at least almost every — member exists, can constructive work be attempted. Even under the best of circumstances, leaders of these groups must always remember that while they spend a limited and prescribed time with their groups each week, the participants must work together, interact, try to understand and be understood by each other every day of their working week.

In all groups the leader must be on the alert for the emergence of subgroups, and for their potential effect on the group as a whole. These effects may be temporary or enduring in nature. They may be disregarded or focused on. They may promote the group's development or hinder it. In the team, their emergence is especially significant. Some members may enter the group as part of a sub-group, with axes to grind and specific interests to protect. The entire group may consist of subgroups, or one subgroup may possess such power that it will succeed, at first, in running the show. There will probably be loners, too, either because no subgroup will accept them or because they do not feel the need or desire to belong to one. Actually, leaders can benefit from these complexities if they do not feel overly threatened by them and can remain open and authentic. If they can be frank about the undertones in their groups that they do not completely grasp and if they can ask for clarification, members will furnish varied perceptions that will help, and, even more important, will teach the participants that others see things very differently from themselves. Indeed, participants may have worked side by side for years without realizing how varied their perceptions are. The there and then has been transformed into the here and now.

SELF-EXPLORATION AND FEEDBACK:
A FIRST GLIMPSE

Joe Luft and Harry Ingham devised a four-panel hypothetical window, called the "Johari window," in an ingenious attempt to help group members better understand themselves and each other (Luft, 1970). I have found their formulation very apt, and I should like to expand on it somewhat before concluding the present introductory chapter.

Of the window's four panes, the first is transparent. Through it I can see certain aspects of myself and my behavior just as others see them. The second quadrant is clear to others but curtained off from my awareness. Through it they perceive a portion of me and my behavior to which I am blind. Through the third square I can look out but others cannot look in. Here, they are shut off from what goes on within me because what is there I hide from them. The fourth pane is opaque to others as well as to myself. It consists of unconscious material of which I am totally or partially unaware and so, of course, are they. Luft and Ingham deal with the first three quadrants only, as the fourth is properly dealt with in deep dyadic therapy. I shall follow in their footsteps.

The first quadrant need hardly concern us. It consists of an ordinary clear windowpane. After all, there are aspects of my personality and behavior that are perceived by others much as I perceive them myself. The outside world cannot further enlighten me here nor I it. The two really important quadrants for the group member, then, remain the second and third.

To some of our behaviors we are blind — and deaf as well. Others see me as fidgeting when I had thought I was calm. Others hear me attacking Jim when I thought I was only setting him right. Still others in the group claim I looked depressed when Alice spoke about her parents — but I had felt nothing. The group insists I interrupt members frequently; I have not been aware of this, believing I hear them out and only react in turn.

As for the third windowpane, it is true that I hide certain things from others. I don't kid myself but just don't share everything with other people. I feel ashamed of part of my past and rather guilty about some of the things I have done or only thought of doing. I even feel shame and guilt about some of my dreams. I am afraid of losing my job and am so nervous that I make one mistake after another at work. I don't know whether to confide in the group. They probably wouldn't understand me and couldn't care less. I'm not sure I can trust them, and, in any case, what good would it do merely to unburden myself?

This third quadrant might be labeled **self-exploration,** whereas the second one might be called **feedback.** In counseling and therapy groups especially, but in other group-work settings as well, self-exploration and feedback are central foci in the ongoing process. Learning from self-exploration involves the willingness to expose oneself verbally to oneself and others. To learn from feedback involves a readiness to face what other group members see in us, hear through us, and sense about us.

We all seem to possess a strong need to be listened to, and, when listening to others in the group, often realize that we are not alone in our anxieties; others also sense in themselves something of what is going on in us. We also note that some things that upset others do not bother us in the least, and of course the contrary is true. After a while, I learn in the group that it is possible to see things from a different angle than that from which I have been viewing matters if, and this is a considerable if, I can bring myself to explore some of my concerns in and with the group. Some time later I may learn that I need not hang on to all of my defenses, although some of them are essential to me. I rationalize less, confront and cope more. And I discover that the feedback that is coming through is not so threatening after all. In any case, it is shifting. Some members are beginning to see me differently. I feel communality within the group but wide divergences as well.

While writing the above, I have not forgotten you, the new group leader. There will be much for you to do, but you must realize from the first that you are not and need not be omniscient. Helping members to explore themselves and giving and receiving meaningful feedback are some of the major tasks. But as yet we have no group. It is time now to consider how groups are formed.

2
Groups Before Action

CLOSED AND OPEN GROUPS

Soon our new group leader will begin to lead a group. Before the group begins, however, let us stop for a while and consider some aspects concerning groups that may seem merely technical but which, in fact, often turn out to be much more than that. Let us begin by looking at closed and open groups.

An **open group** is one whose membership fluctuates during the period of its existence. The setting — room and meeting time — tends to remain fixed. The leader continues to lead the group, but there is a turnover in membership; however, once begun, the group may continue for years. Frequently, open groups are found in hospital and other institutional settings as well as in child guidance clinics. Thus, for example, in a halfway house for mental patients there may be a group in which clients discuss, learn about, and face their strengths and weaknesses as they return to the ouside world. There is a waiting list, and as soon as one group member leaves, a new participant takes his or her place. The waiting period may be long or short, depending on the particular circumstances of each group. Chances are, however, that if candidates had to wait for the organization of a new group, the time would be much longer.

The **closed group,** on the other hand, may be closed from its very first meeting. If not, it will become so after the membership settles down — usually no later than the third session. Once members have been selected for the group, agree to participate, and actually appear, the group closes its doors. Nowadays, there is a great proliferation of closed groups. They are found in various institutions and agencies, schools, industry, government, and so forth. It is obvious that leaders of closed groups must select their participants carefully because, if members drop out, they cannot easily be replaced. This, in addition to reducing group number, may hurt group morale. Meanwhile, the waiting list for potential group candidates lengthens.

The open group, by definition, cannot develop an unbroken history. As members leave and others join the group its dynamics may change radically. Yet the membership tends to be stable long enough that some group cohesion develops and certain group forces can be identified and analyzed. Open groups generally stress individual learnings in a group setting in which these learnings predominate and the group as such is secondary.

The closed group, once its membership is fixed, becomes in fact a microsociety and begins to develop its own history. Members are launched on a joint venture. In this particular milieu, the group and its dynamics can be dealt with in depth but the group itself will decide whether to emphasize group or individual learnings. As far as termination of such a group is concerned, this may be determined before it begins to function. Alternatively, the group may be empowered to make the decision for itself.

I have worked with both open and closed groups and well realize that there is room for each. I, myself, prefer the closed group but admit that this is only a personal inclination. Neophytes should become familiar with the workings of both. Should they develop a particular taste for group dynamics, chances are that they will also opt for the closed group whenever possible.

THE SETTING

To most of us, a clearly defined setting provides security and certainty. So much in the group's life will be vague, confusing, and constantly changing that we must take steps to provide at least a clearly defined setting. By this I do not wish to imply that leaders should be arbitrary or rigid. If members' preferences can be accommodated so much the better, but once a setting is fixed leaders should consider themselves responsible for its maintenance.

In connection with this, new group leaders should be cognizant of certain pitfalls. They may at first have such a strong need to be liked and thought well of by members that they are tempted to agree to a setting inconvenient for them personally or, in their judgment, unsuitable for the group. Thus, for example, even though a leader and supervisor have scheduled group meetings for Wednesdays at six in the evening, taking into account their own schedules, the availability of rooms, equipment, and so forth, the neophyte may consent under slight group pressure to transfer the meetings to Tuesdays, knowing well that this will be most inconvenient personally and perhaps impossible for the supervisor, who has agreed to observe early meetings from the observation booth.

The group and its leader require a room that is always at their disposal for scheduled meetings. This room should be adequately furnished with comfortable chairs and any equipment the leader intends to use, and it should be situated in a relatively quiet area. Needless to say, the group's privacy must be ensured, as there will be enough frustration generated without the added disturbance of outsiders intruding.

In group life as in everyday life, time is an important dimension. Much of our daily existence is regulated by the clock. We work during specific hours of the day, and many of our recreational activities are scheduled, as is our transportation. Children and adults must learn to adjust themselves to time. Some do so compulsively, others nonchalantly, and still others rebelliously. Be this as it may, if group meetings have been planned for Wednesday evening from six to seven-thirty, the plan should be followed as closely as possible. If the leader takes it seriously, members will learn to do so as well, and the group will tend to start closer to six than to six-twenty. I am concerned even more, however, about closing on time.

As you will soon discover, a certain rhythm characterizes group life at every meeting. It will probably take the group a few minutes to get started while greetings are exchanged, the chitchat dies down, and latecomers are seated. The group will then turn its attention to work. Tensions may build up, self-explorations be attempted, feedback be given, and confrontations occur. Since, generally speaking, members will not meet for another week, the group should not end on a high note. It is up to the leader to conduct the orchestra in such a way that new themes are not introduced too late in any particular session, so that the meeting may end much as it began — on a relatively muted note and more or less punctually. New themes brought in toward the end should by no means be ignored. They should, however, be postponed until the next session, when the leader will have to decide whether to reintroduce them or wait and see whether the member in question or someone else does so. I have come across group participants who so consistently brought up issues late in the meeting that everyone else in the group was aware that they could not then be worked on. It always proved helpful to point this out and suggest what this might mean while, nonetheless, finishing the meeting as scheduled. Should vital matters that demand a longer session arise, the group may be prepared to forego individual plans and commitments and prolong the meeting for once. However, flexibility can be learned and practiced only where a basic structure exists.

I very much believe in group life but not at all in "groupiness." Structure and setting should be utilized to protect the former and guard against the latter. Group life is fostered by neutral surroundings and fixed meeting hours. Within this framework, group history will unfold and the group will work toward goals. Groupiness tends to develop when members perceive as all important the perpetuation of the group rather than the furthering of its specific learning goals. It will lead to meetings in members' homes, in restaurants, and other public places. Should members decide to meet outside the group setting, that is their own private concern, but this socializing should by no means be equated with the learning goals of the group. If the group meets socially and invites the leader, he or she may certainly accept the invitation, but as a guest and not in the role of group leader.

Regarding the setting-connected issues of group frequency, attendance, and duration, the leader must take into account, among other factors, the goals of the group. If the dynamics of group life are to be deeply experienced and examined, meetings should take place at least once weekly for no less than an hour and a half. Groups that meet twice a week can, of course, delve even more deeply into personal and group dynamics. Meeting every two weeks performs primarily a maintenance and didactic function. A group that meets twice monthly can function well within a discussion format, where the leader or a member introduces a topic that is followed, perhaps, by a lecture and then a discussion. It can also function usefully as a guidance group in which the leader performs the role of the expert, assisting individual members with their problems on the assumption that this will benefit other members as well. In this framework, participants may certainly ask questions and interact briefly with the leader or each other, but the goal remains guidance. By no means do I wish to denigrate such groups, for they fulfill an important task in our society. However, their limited goals must be recognized for what they are; if clients need more than what is provided, they should be supported in that direction.

In all groups, member attendance at times presents a problem. Someone may know in advance that he or she will not be able to attend a meeting and may feel that this should be explained to the leader. After that member returns, another member may attempt to excuse an absence to the leader. Once a group is actually functioning, I believe such matters should be referred to the group, rather than to the leader. If this practice is consistently followed, members will learn to face the group directly. Should absenteeism become prevalent, the leader has to ask him- or herself and the group members what lies behind it. Not all groups succeed and not all that fail do so because of the leader.

Finally, concerning the duration of groups, there are no clear-cut criteria. Group life is similar to individual life insofar as much can be accomplished in a short period, while a longer one may at times be unproductive. Frequently, because of agency policy, vacation schedules, or theoretical considerations, members are informed in advance of the duration of a particular group. The timetable should be honored. However, before termination, members should discuss the rationale of the scheduling and evaluate its justification in terms of group needs. When group duration has not been determined in advance, the group should meet as long as it is doing useful work together and no longer. It is the responsibility of the leader to see to it that members do not become too dependent either on the leader or on the group itself. I am opposed to addiction, even in the form of groups.

GROUP COMPOSITION AND SIZE

The factors of correct composition and size of a group, in my opinion, are more a matter of what *feels* right than of what *is* right. I even doubt that there exists a right size or a correct composition. The general rule regarding size that works for me cautions that when in doubt, take more rather than fewer members. Absences will certainly occur and there may be dropouts, too. Even under the best of circumstances, people fall ill or move away. I personally feel very comfortable with a group of twelve but also feel at ease with fifteen or, for that matter, with ten. If interpersonal competence and communication is a goal of the group, I want few enough members so that this type of interaction can take place, and yet enough members so that everyone can allow him- or herself to sit back occasionally and just observe the interaction of others without the work of the group being impaired.

At times, group size is a given. I have consulted with committees of four and worked with teams of twenty. The inexperienced group leader, I strongly suspect, should not work with very small groups — by which I mean under ten members. The smaller the group, the more active the leader will have to be and the more will be expected. As the old adage puts it, there is safety in numbers, and the insecure neophyte will justifiably prefer as much safety as possible.

Another general rule I have set for myself is that when the members themselves are the focus of attention, the group should be smaller than when the focus is on persons external to the group: members' children, members' clients, and so forth. If I meet on a weekly basis with a parents' group to discuss their difficulties with offspring, or with a group of beginning counselors interested in exploring certain aspects of work with their clients, I can easily work with eighteen. Incidentally, it has been my experience that the exercise of confidentiality is not a function of group size. I have known both large and small groups that decided to keep the content of their sessions confidential and have seen the same proportion of success and failure in maintaining this norm.

Regarding group composition, you will find in the literature, in theory and in practice, justification for almost any combination you can think of. Let me point out, however, that frequently you will have no real choice. You may, for example, prefer to have both sexes represented in your groups. This becomes something of a problem in a male ward or an institution for wayward girls. You may wish both fathers and mothers to attend your parents' group, but if your agency functions only during the day, you will most likely find that only mothers attend sessions. But if you set up a group specifically intended to confront men and women, minority and majority sectors, teachers and pupils, union and management, or any similar arrangement, participants should be represented in more or less equal numbers. Twelve Jews and two Arabs or the reverse make the achievement of better interpersonal relations among them doubtful from the very beginning. I have found that in groups dealing with majority-minority issues, the ratio of six to four seems to work very well.

It is not desirable to mix total strangers with members who are well acquainted with each other. This tends to set up two sub-groups from the very start, subgroups that have not formed as the result of group development. It sometimes happens that in a group designed for strangers, two or three people turn out to be ac-quainted with one another. If this does not bother them, it need not disturb anyone else. But the matter must be checked out, since al-though the presence of B may not bother A, A's presence may cause B great unease. In this case it is best to adopt a solution that enables one of them to remain, the other to leave, and both not to resent it.

When the group consists of people who work for the same com-pany, naturally all the participants know each other well. I have already discussed in Chapter 1 the need to handle such groups care-fully. What needs to be stressed about group composition is that should the "boss," "head," or supervisor — in short, the person in charge of the team — not be included among the participants, you would do well to refuse to work with the team. With the authority figure absent you may expect, in members' projections at the very least, to become a handy substitute. Things will be stated or hinted about the team's leader that cannot be checked out without that person being there. Without the boss, issues in which he or she is involved cannot in many instances be tackled. Much less can they be resolved. On the other hand, absent chiefs may suspect plots against them. Their presence, will not simplify group life, especially if relations between them and the rest of the team are distant or strained, but it is still far better to have supervisors there so that improvements in work relations may be attempted with all con-cerned parties participating. Even if you should conclude that legiti-mate, objective reasons prevent the team leader from participating, be careful; the odds are against you.

Finally, where it is possible to screen potential members, I sug-gest that beginners, in particular, include a few "talkers" in their groups. Verbal people can rather easily be detected during the selec-tion process. They are not always helpful to the group but they con-siderably cut down those awful silences that are the bane of the neophyte. However, do everything possible to avoid being saddled with too many aggressive members. Unfortunately, open, verbal aggression is not always apparent before the group begins to work, but should you discover that too many aggressive members have been included and you are finding it too difficult to cope, try to change the group's composition before serious work starts.

What about group leaders themselves? How do they fit into the picture? Essentially, competent group leaders should be able to function adequately in any group, whatever its composition, that deals with matters in which they are professionally trained. I have seen diminutive women operate successfully as group leaders of work teams composed of husky men. Age may sometimes be a factor worth considering. I, myself, prefer not to work with adolescents — I look like their grandfather. But this is undoubtedly my personal hang-up, as I know leaders my age who do very well with that age group. Still, it is probably best for young neophytes not to begin with groups whose members could easily be their fathers or mothers.

SEATING

Since most interactions in the groups we are considering are verbal and take place while everyone is seated, seating is by no means the trivial matter it might appear to be at first glance. Comfortable chairs should be available for all. By this I do not mean luxurious chairs, but simply comfortable ones — and, I repeat, for everyone. If there are just a few, who sits on what chair may unnecessarily become an issue that might, of course, be used therapeutically — but surely more relevant topics can be discovered. No special chairs should be provided for leader or observer as this also can set off an authority game that could be played more profitably on other grounds. Speaking from personal preference, I suggest that the leader not occupy the same seat session after session — and this not because I wish to obscure the leadership role. Rather, a leader's moving about from session to session will encourage others to do likewise. Thus members may intermingle more than they might otherwise, and the group setting will be more flexible. At the very least, the leader is not inviting rigidity. If the leader works with a co-leader and/or observer, they should not sit in close proximity to one another, lest the group suspect collusion.

I do not believe the group, of necessity, must sit in a circle. Any arrangement will do, so long as all present sit in such a way that everyone can see the facial expression of everyone else. The meeting room should not be so small that participants sit practically one on top of the other. We rightly wish to respect our clients; therefore, we certainly should respect their personal space as well. Some members need more private space than others; they are entitled to it. When I have to choose between a room that is too small and one that is too large, I always opt for the larger one. After all, we need not occupy all of it and, at least, we shall not feel hemmed in.

Should the group sit around a table? Generally speaking, I am opposed to this arrangement. Although the group's main interaction is verbal, many nonverbal cues will get lost under or behind the table. Furthermore, the group may engage in various exercises that require moving about: dividing up into small teams, changing seats during a session for more effective role-playing, and so on. In any of these instances, the table will interfere. Ashtrays, handbags, and other such items can be put on the floor. Should tables be insisted on, I suggest small, low ones that can be placed between chairs.

What about eating during group sessions? To this I am adamantly opposed. If members wish to have a snack or drink coffee together, encourage them to do this before or after sessions. The meeting itself should be devoted to the task at hand.

There is probably some significance in where people choose to sit, but I, for one, must admit that it eludes me. I used to subscribe to various theories about those who tended to sit to my right or left or directly across from me, but I have given these up. However, especially in a group whose seating pattern tends to change, it is interesting to observe who sits near whom most of the time and who never gets close to whom. Again, I do not vouch for deep significance but am prepared to check things out if I have a hunch it might be useful to the group or, at least, to some part of it. I feel rather certain of one thing, though: it is dangerous to attribute too much meaning to the seating pattern of the first session as much of it may be no more than pure accident.

LET'S NOT GO AROUND THE CIRCLE

This section is going to be very brief, and if it figures as a section at all it is because I feel so strongly about the matter. I simply hate it when, as the result of a suggestion from the leader or a member, everyone, in turn, is required to express an opinion or feeling regarding a particular subject. I find that this "going around the circle" is most uncongenial, to say the least. It forces members to speak when some may prefer, just then, to remain silent. It encourages them to prepare in advance what they are going to say when their turn arrives, rather than to listen to what others are saying. It contradicts much of what we wish to teach in most groups: to speak freely and spontaneously, to listen to others as sensitively as possible, and to work in a warm, flexible climate suited to all members' needs. So, let's not go around the circle.

THE GROUP THAT MEETS ONLY ONCE

Rarely is a group formed for just one meeting, but it does happen. Such meetings are often connected with exploring a certain project, demonstrating a way of working with groups, or planning for possible joint action at some future time. In such cases, leaders must do everything within their power in order, at the very least, not to leave so negative an impression with members that they may not wish to join a group of any kind for a long time afterward. On the positive side, leaders must see to it that meetings are clearly structured and the setting well defined. Probing in depth should be avoided. Leaders will want to check very carefully whether they have understood participants well and have, in turn, been understood by them. Toward the end, a summary of the discussion may prove helpful to all concerned. Possible misunderstandings should be cleared up before the meeting is brought to a close.

In connection with this, I should like to give an illustration. Some time ago I was contacted by the principal of a large secondary school in order to look into the possibility of helping the system initiate an organization development program. A meeting was scheduled with a group of senior teachers and administrative staff. We met in the principal's office at a convenient time when school was not in session. The principal led the meeting itself, whereas I initiated the discussion pertaining to the project. After I had presented a short exposition, many questions were posed and doubts expressed. Toward the end of the meeting, we summarized the alternative lines of action proposed, the points on which we agreed, and those on which some of us differed. Divergences of opinion among the members were clearly stated, and although I thought I sensed that some felt threatened, others anxious, and a few enthusiastic, I believed it best to keep these impressions to myself for the time being. Once the project got under way, I did not meet again with that particular group.

LEADER INTERVENTIONS

In this chapter I have discussed at some length many of the varied and more-or-less technical interventions in group life that leaders must be prepared to make. Before concluding, however, I wish merely to hint at the more meaningful interventions leaders will have to master when functioning in ongoing groups. I do so primarily for the sake of balance, as these will be discussed more fully later on.

Leaders may intervene on the **content** level — what is actually being said cognitively. In this context, leaders may wish to state their own opinions, present research findings, or provide other information related to the discussion. They may, perhaps, decide to lecture briefly on a theoretical aspect relevant to their groups' present needs and development. At other times, leaders may disregard content entirely and suggest that their groups focus on **process** — what is going on in the groups as a whole, among particular members, between subgroups, with one particular individual. They may inquire what members see happening or present their own perceptions and ask for comments. Leaders may wish to know how group members perceive leader behavior at any given moment.

A leader may give the group specific directions such as:
> We'll have to stop soon for today. Perhaps someone would like to sum up our discussion.

Or the leader might try a different approach:
> John and Sue, you seem to be having an interesting chat. How about sharing some of it with the rest of us.

On the other hand, leaders may ask for and actively encourage the expression of feelings. They may express their own feelings in order to show that this need not be threatening, and that the expression of one's own feelings is legitimate.

A leader, for example, may decide to focus on Jim, talking to him as if the group were not present, as if the two were in a dyadic relationship for the moment. The leader may wish to empathize with Jim, confirm whether Jim has been understood properly, confront him on an issue — all this in order to help Jim as well as provide a behavior model for the group. The leader may feel it necessary to intervene, on occasion, in order to protect Betty when the leader feels that the group is being too harsh with her, using her as a scapegoat, or putting her on the spot more than is warranted. The leader may wish to check out with the group how members feel about this intervention, and will, perhaps, react to their reactions.

Finally, leaders may decide to give direct feedback to their groups as a whole or to a specific participant. They will then want to ascertain how they were understood and learn how the feedback was received. Leaders may also request feedback regarding the behavior of the entire group, that of a given member, or their own. At this point leaders may wish to present their views on helpful, as opposed to harmful, feedback.

3
Nightmare and Reality

FINAL PREPARATIONS
FOR THE FIRST MEETING

Let us accompany Gloria Brown and Bill Thomas as they prepare for their first group meeting. Both are well-trained professionals and feel comfortable in their jobs. Gloria Brown is a psychologist at a child guidance clinic, and Bill Thomas is a social worker on the staff of a large rehabilitation center for the blind. Both know about groups from several college courses, additional random reading, and from participation in a T-Group run by a reputable training institute. Both want very much to try their hand at group work. They feel more or less ready — they know there has to be a first time someday — and now their chance has arrived.

Gloria is about to begin a parents' group, a group for parents whose children are being seen at the clinic. Some time ago she received a list of potential candidates from her coworkers. She decided to interview them all on an individual basis. In this one-time dyadic interview, she would become acquainted with each candidate and gather enough of an impression to enable her to decide, taking into account additional information from the file, whether or not to include that individual in the group. In addition, she also hoped to be able to answer the interviewee's questions about the projected group and to provide necessary information regarding goals and setting. She had considered interviewing candidates in one large group or a few smaller groups in order to see how they interacted, and also to save time, but was now pleased she had rejected that plan. In the dyadic interview, she had been able to talk things over leisurely with each parent, and as far as group interaction was concerned, that would come in its turn.

Among the candidates, Gloria also interviewed some of her own clients whom she considered suitable for the group. The fact that she knew them much better than the other participants would not, she believed, hamper the situation. Her clients thought this would not disturb them either and agreed that she tell the group of their prior relationship. Almost by chance, she discovered that several candidates living in the same district knew each other. One preferred to wait until another group was set up, in order to be with strangers. The screening and selection proceeded smoothly. Two candidates decided against joining the group, whereas a third was only willing to try it. Gloria felt sure that she had some real talkers and no one unduly aggressive on her list. Since the group would have to meet during the day, few fathers could attend. After a last-minute cancellation, she was now about to begin her first group meeting with twelve mothers and three fathers. She was aware of the possibility that others might drop out. The group was intended to be a closed one and to run for about a year.

Bill's situation was quite different. At the most recent staff meeting of the center for the blind, it had been decided to set up a group for those trainees who were to be discharged within the next six weeks — an idea long contemplated but somehow never attempted till now. The group would meet twice a week in the early afternoon. It would deal with the rehabilitants' immediate and longer-range plans for when they left the Center, as well as their fears, anxieties, hopes, and expectations about these plans. This first attempt at a group for "graduates" would include six males and five females, ranging in age from eighteen to sixty.

Bill was delighted with his assignment. He was relatively new at the Center, but he already knew all of the candidates. They, of course, were well acquainted with each other, having spent a considerable amount of time together. Bill assembled the candidates, informed them of the staff's decision, and invited comment. As he had expected, it was mixed. After listening to them all, he suggested that they thrash out their feelings and reactions more fully at the first meeting, scheduled for the following afternoon, and asked if anyone was prepared to open. Two volunteers agreed to think about it. Bill was not sure that everyone would actively participate or, for that matter, attend, but he was ready to discover what could be accomplished.

THE NIGHTMARE

The evening before the first parents' group meeting, Gloria had a nightmare. She could and did laugh when she related it later, but while it was happening there was nothing at all funny about the dream. She recalled the panic she felt as she sat in the meeting room waiting, waiting, and no one, no one at all showed up. She sat there all alone until suddenly she heard voices. Someone was remarking that of course no one would come to *her* group; it would only be a waste of time — what could they possibly learn? Then they were all sitting in the room with her, staring and waiting. Not a sound was uttered. She tried to smile, to say something, to get them, to get anyone to talk. When they finally did, they all screamed at each other, at their children, and at her. And then she found herself screaming, too: they could all go back where they had come from, she did not need them, she was not going to be their father or mother figure or any other figure. . . . In a flood of guilt and shame she implored forgiveness and understanding. After all, she was new at this and . . . They wouldn't tell her colleagues, would they? They glared at her until she burst into tears. One of the mothers began to speak. She talked and talked. People asked her to stop, demanded that Gloria shut her up, but she just talked on and on. Suddenly Gloria's supervisor appeared, pointed an accusing finger at her and the assembled members, laughed eerily, and left. The group then rose in a body and ran out of the room as well. Gloria was alone again, all alone, and it was awful! Then, shivering and soaked in perspiration, she awoke.

THE REALITY

Of course, things turned out very differently. What Gloria remembered best about that first meeting was that she felt in control of the situation most of the time, and that people liked her. She recognized some of her mistakes even as she was making them. For one thing she talked too much, and most of the interaction seemed to be channeled through her rather than among the members, but she did not know yet how to change this. For another, she had forgotten to mention that she was acquainted with some of the members from previous contacts in the Clinic. This, however, did not bother her too much. What did annoy her considerably was that she just did not know how to bring the meeting to a close. There *was* real interaction going on by closing time, and most members were absorbed, but a few were glancing at their watches, and outside others were waiting impatiently for the room. Someone had actually opened the door and peeked in. As for being liked, she knew she was likable and felt friendly toward people. During the session she had noted glances and smiles in her direction. This had given her assurance and confidence. She hoped not too much hostility would appear in the group. She knew she would have trouble handling it.

Bill experienced no nightmare the night before his first group session; as a matter of fact, he never dreamed at all. The meeting itself had gone off passably enough. Just as he had anticipated, John had not showed up, which he felt was probably no loss as he might well have disrupted everything. Although members were well acquainted with each other, it had been difficult for them to get started. Perhaps he hadn't helped enough, had been too passive. Aside from the members' blindness, they did not actually have too much in common. Archie seemed very concerned about landing a job, and Betty expressed doubt as to whether she would make it through college. But the others did not always seem to be paying attention. Bill did not grasp what all the joking and horseplay was about. Perhaps two meetings a week would be too much for some of them. He thought he would like to talk to members individually and try to get more reactions. He certainly hadn't felt much enthusiasm in the group. Perhaps he himself could have done more to generate it, but he had felt somehow left out of things. He would have to look into that.

Both Gloria and Bill knew after their first group session — in a way they had never experienced it before — that they still had a great deal to learn. Gloria was glad that her supervisor had observed the session from behind the one-way screen — at least now that it was over. During the session itself she had occasionally glanced at the mirror, wondering. In any case, she was sorry that no one had been available to co-lead with her. Perhaps with the next group she would have a co-leader. Bill was less fortunate. A one-way mirror had not yet been installed at the Center, and his supervisor was on vacation. Well, he would write up the meeting as best he could and wait for his return.

Under more or less favorable circumstances, Bill and Gloria and many like them will learn and make progress and feel increasingly at home with their groups. They will learn to live more comfortably with the idea that they are looked on as behavior models, model setters, and authority figures. They will recognize that each group develops at its own pace and that group development cannot be forced. Neither can the self-exploration or self-disclosure of members be forced; it cannot be forced in a dyadic relationship either. New leaders will learn to acknowledge errors — first to themselves, then to their supervisors and, finally, to their groups. Once a neophyte can admit to the members of the group that he or she has erred — not in order to curry favor, to earn sympathy, or to be accepted as another fallible member, but simply because it is human to err — the neophyte is no longer just another beginner.

FINDING YOUR OWN GROUP

It goes without saying that your legitimate, long-range objective as a new group leader is to be able eventually to lead groups in your own way, in your own style, and at your own pace. But this goal cannot be achieved overnight. It takes much practice, reflection, and experience — especially the last. Until you discover your own style, you will probably copy that of others, or think you are copying them. You will experiment with various behaviors until you latch onto those that are really you. One day you will be sure of yourself, the next somewhat confused, and totally lost the day after that. You will try out new and different procedures until you discover those that work best for you. You will talk, eat, and dream groups until things fall into a pattern, and you can begin to relax. You will wish you had never started with groups and you will contemplate working only with groups — until you hit upon the balance best for you.

The only meaningful suggestion I can offer along this road is this: join your own group. In a way, I am telling you to practice what you preach. You explain to potential members of your groups what a group has to offer, what is unique about a group experience, and how it might help them. All of this, and more, applies in your own case as well. The group I have in mind and have seen in action is composed of neophytes like yourself, led by one or two experienced group leaders. It meets at least once a week and may go on meeting for months. Its primary goal is to help you become as effective a group leader as you can and learn to do *your* thing, not that of anyone else.

Gloria and Bill joined such a group. Here the neophytes exchanged feelings and impressions about their unfamiliar leader role, while at the same time experiencing what it is like to be a group member. It was in this group that Gloria related her nightmare and Bill spoke of his feeling that the group of rehabilitants had kept him at arm's length. It was here that, in time, they grew and developed as group leaders.

4
The Group Meets

THE GROUP BEGINS

I think every group leader feels a certain excitement when beginning a new group; I know I do. With all that we know theoretically
about groups, practically about our own profession, and experien-
tially about group life, we meet this specific new group as though
it were for the first time. And, in a way, it is. With these potential
members, with this very particular group that is molding itself
right under your eyes — right under your baton as it were — with
this group, in fact, you begin again. They have either approached
you to lead them, or else you have, as a member of an organization
or in a private capacity, suggested to them that they participate.
Whatever the case, here they are. They seem excited, too, a bit
tense, some of them a bit stiff, others a little too nonchalant, looking at you, and waiting for your first move. They attempt to seem
relaxed. Some are reading, others seem to be resting, some are exchanging pleasantries. But you are not taken in by this seeming
calm. They are still looking at you; they are waiting for you to
speak. And so, as you feel your heart quickening at the excitement
of another human encounter, you clear your throat and begin.

You do the most obvious thing first, you introduce yourself —
but what do you say to people you have already met, if even only
once? In any case, just what *is* your name right now? Should a
psychiatrist in the out-patient clinic of a hospital, some of whose
clients are now sitting in front of him, be called Dr. Joseph Smith
or Joe or Mr. Smith or Dr. Smith or Joe Smith? He will have to
decide. Whatever you decide in your own case is probably a function of your personality, of how much you value your professional
affiliation, of the culture in which you live, of the norms of your
particular institution, and of your picture of your role as the group
leader. There is really no one right way. I suspect that in England
you would introduce yourself by your surname and whatever pro-

fessional title you have, and would assume that members would address each other by surname. In the United States you might assume that members will call each other by their given names from the start. I have encountered all the permutations. In our example the group leader introduced himself as Dr. Smith, but within a few sessions members were addressing him as Joe or else without any name at all. It was that kind of group and he was that kind of leader.

Consider Professor Robert Jones, an organization development consultant specializing in education. He was asked to consult with a certain school district in his city. It was decided to set up a steering committee that would meet with him over a number of weeks. He met all of the members of the committee, interviewed some of them, and talked informally with others. So, when they got together for the first meeting of the group, he introduced himself as Bob, assuming that first names would be used all around. And so they were, but, as it turned out, most of the members kept referring to Bob as Professor Jones. That is the kind of group it was and the kind of leader they perceived him to be.

Should you relate anything more about yourself? Again, that is entirely up to you. I can only suggest that if you do, it should be brief. Some leaders like to say a word about their professional background and affiliations, their experience with groups, their age, marital status, and so forth. Others prefer to add nothing personal at this point. I find myself in a somewhat difficult position here since I happen to be blind. If I do not inform the group of this disability at the outset, misunderstandings might arise. If I do mention it, people might be shocked or, at least, feel uncomfortable. I prefer to tell. Some people know anyway, but I decided a long time ago that they should all hear it from me, simply and directly. As for the shock and possible uneasiness, they are present at times, but have never proved to be insurmountable obstacles. I hope I am not fooling myself.

Leaders may wish to express at this time personal feelings about their hopes for and expectations of their groups.

Dr. Smith said:

> I hope we can learn to get along together and perhaps even to like one another. I expect that in time you'll be able to be frank and open in the group. I shall try to be the same.

Bob expressed his feelings this way:

> We are going to work hard here and, at the same time,
> I hope, have fun together. You know your system and
> I don't. I hope you'll set me straight whenever I go
> off tangent. Please be honest with me and with each
> other.

At this point I feel it is important to structure the setting once
again and, briefly, to restate the purpose and goals of the group.
Joe Smith said that the group would meet every Monday evening
from seven-thirty to nine, and that new members would be admitted from time to time as present members left the group. The
group was meeting to help people with their social interactions so
that "we can learn to function more adequately at work and at
home." Bob Jones pointed out to the steering committee that it had
been agreed to get together weekly on Thursdays for lunch and an
early afternoon session lasting until three o'clock. It was his understanding that the purpose of the meetings was to improve interpersonal communication among the members, in order, eventually,
to improve the channels of communication within the school
district.

The entire monologue should not take more than a very few
minutes. Now the leader should pause and invite reactions and
comments. Although, from the leader's vantage point, everything
is perfectly clear, it may not be so to all members. There may be
questions and comments about matters totally unrelated to what
has just been said. The leader will have to decide to what to reply
and to what to react, but should certainly not give any members
the feeling that they have not been heard, even if, for the moment,
they do not receive answers. If nothing is forthcoming from the
group, the leader should move on to the next item on the agenda,
for at this point long silence would be meaningless and frustrating,
and is totally unnecessary.

Now the leader should state, briefly but clearly, his or her perceptions of the leader's role in the group. These may be forgotten
along the way and have to be repeated on future occasions, but it
is, I feel, important to present them right at the beginning. Dr.
Smith put it this way:

> As for my role here, I want you to know that I don't
> have all the answers. I make mistakes like anyone
> else. I'll try to tell you what I see going on in the

group and how I see each of you behaving. I hope we
can learn together what this means to us here in this
room, and what it might mean for each of you on the
outside — in your family life, at work, with your
friends. If you decide to change some of your behaviors, that's up to you and if you don't, that's also up
to you. . . . Who wants to start?

Professor Jones defined his role as process consultant to the committee. He might have expanded on that, but someone wanted to
say something right then, so he decided that further explanations
of his role, if indeed necessary, could wait. The group was under
way. Jones did not have to help this group to begin work. The
members of the committee were experienced professionals and were
ready for action.

Unfortunately, groups do not always get off to such an easy
start. After Joe Smith had stopped talking, the room fell silent.
People looked out the window, at the ceiling, at their shoes. Ciga-
rettes were lit and chairs scraped, but no one spoke. Joe was not
disconcerted. He had seen this happen in many a group. After a
short pause he suggested that people might want to introduce
themselves. That broke the ice. One by one, members volunteered
basic information. Then again there was silence. This time Joe
waited a bit longer. As he was about to turn to Mary and tell her
he had noticed that she had just lit her third cigarette, Jim spoke
up. Another group had been launched.

BRINGING THE SESSION TO A CLOSE

If getting a group session going is sometimes difficult, bringing it
to a close is often even harder. The group leader must be aware of
time; it is one of the important dimensions of group structure. I
have already explained why, in my opinion, it is so essential to end
on time. By this I do not mean obsessively on the second, but,
rather, within a reasonable leeway. It is perfectly fitting, I think,
to end a few minutes earlier if the group has come to a good stop-
ping point. It is bad for everyone concerned to drag the meeting
on and on merely because no one, including the leader, knows how

to bring it to an end. Just the other day in one of my groups, when I felt the session was running down, I said something like:

> It looks like nobody wants to add anything to what Hannah has said. Am I right? ... [silence] ... Well, in that case, let's call it a day. No use starting on something new at this hour.

As in a sonata, any new theme introduced in a group requires development before it is even superficially understood. For genuine understanding to occur, communication will have to take place. The speaker may elaborate on the theme. Others may contribute comments, clarifications, questions, counterthemes of their own. It is a pity to cut off this interplay, and doing so may be harmful to the group. Therefore, some leaders are stymied when they lose touch with time. New material has been introduced, and while it unfolds the group becomes conflicted. Participants want to hear Jim out; others want their say, too, but must leave. Some have a class to attend, others a train to catch, and the leader is already late for a next appointment. All this can be rather easily avoided.

But what if new material has been introduced at the last minute anyway? This certainly does occur at times, and when it does, the best way out is the simple truth:

> I'm glad you brought up this matter about your mother and you, June. It would be a good idea to start with it next meeting. We all have to rush off soon, and wouldn't want to leave you stranded in the middle.

This cutting off can seem cruel at times, especially when it happens to a relatively nonverbal member. But what is the alternative? If everyone, for once, could stay an extra quarter of an hour or so, it might be worthwhile, but the leader will have to make a quick decision — if the matter were put to the group, it might take all that time just to decide, and by then everyone would really have to leave. Another alternative would be to encourage June at the start of the next session to begin again. This will show her, at least, that the leader remembers. Still another possibility is for the leader to approach June after the meeting, restate the regret the leader expressed in the group, and ask what she would prefer: to bring up the subject next time or to await a cue from someone in the group.

The cruelest thing, I am certain, would be to ignore the time factor for the moment, and let June become involved in her story, only to realize that people are not really paying attention.

A certain type of participant will unfailingly introduce new material toward the end of sessions. This compulsion presents a special problem that must be dealt with in terms of the leader's perceptions of the specific member; there may be some deep-lying difficulty. In any event, the phenomenon should by no means be ignored, but should be responded to firmly and sensitively. A one-time individual meeting might be indicated if the group cannot cope with the problem.

I consider it best to end most meetings on a downward curve. Group sessions usually begin andante and move on to presto or vivace. They should close with another andante, as, generally, it is not particularly helpful to have people leave in a state of high tension, ruffled feelings, and unspent emotions. It is obviously unavoidable at times and may even help the group move forward, but I still think that most of the time ending on a high emotional level should be avoided. Closure is important in life; it is important in group life as well.

Should an attempt be made to summarize meetings before the group disperses? I do not really know. When learnings are primarily cognitive, a brief summary may be useful. If group members have taken upon themselves certain tasks that they are to carry out before the next meeting, a summary is essential to ensure that all members understand what they are to do. If a member has received a great deal of feedback, it might be profitable to have the person summarize it. If certain group learnings have occurred that the leader wishes to collate in a summary statement, the leader may opt to do so toward the end of the meeting. For the rest, I think it is primarily a matter of leader style and member preferences. These will differ from group to group.

Should the next meeting be planned before the present one ends? In therapy and counseling groups I believe this is contraindicated, since spontaneity and the here and now element are essential. What about other groups? Bill Thomas's group worked much more successfully once it had decided that at the beginning of each meeting a member would present a life plan for the coming ten years. Members chose the next "victim" toward the end of every session.

Bob Jones's committee decided that at each of its meetings, in rotation, a member would start by presenting a report on an aspect of the district's educational system about which he or she was particularly knowledgeable. These reports proved so stimulating and comprehensive that they were later edited, mimeographed, and distributed to a wider audience. As for the committee itself, it broke up when the reports were finished.

THE DIARY

Whether the group is open or closed, the group experience itself intensive or superficial, I generally recommend that all participants keep a diary. This diary is theirs to do with as they please, to show to the group, to me, or, if they prefer, to no one. They may wish to read aloud from it during group meetings or decide never to refer to it at any time. Of course, they are fully entitled to reject my suggestion and not keep a diary.

An ordinary notebook is perfectly adequate for the diary, but it must be one that will serve no other purpose. In it members note whatever they wish to about the group and themselves: summaries of interchanges and interactions; new personal learnings — cognitive, emotional, behavioral; general and specific comments on the life of the group, on the leader, and reflections on the shaping of the group's history. I look upon the diary as a personal document of group and individual development, and I suggest keeping one because I consider it important for members to think about their group between meetings, and, at least while it lasts, to make it an important facet of their lives. Diary entries concerning group events are best written as soon as possible after each meeting. They can be based, of course, on brief items jotted down while sessions are in progress. I have known members who declined to make the effort, but have not yet encountered one who kept this kind of diary and regretted it afterwards.

KEEPING RECORDS

Recording does not play the crucial role in the group that it does in the dyadic interview (Benjamin, 1974). Group life is so diffuse, so much takes place simultaneously, so many different and yet valid individual perceptions are generated, that it is extremely difficult to record group life precisely and objectively. But since every group, I maintain, develops its own history, who shall be its historian? First of all, the group members themselves are its historians. Their diaries, if kept as I suggest, provide excellent source material. The leader, the observer, and mechanical devices may contribute additional information.

Should notes be taken during group meetings? I think it preferable that this not be done extensively. However, an occasional jotting down will certainly not disturb the group atmosphere. In most instances, leaders will not want to take more than fleeting notes during group sessions. They are far too involved, and it would be pretty futile for them to attempt comprehensive note taking. If an observer is to take notes while observing, the reason for this procedure must be explained as part of the structure. The notes must be seen as the property of the particular group, to be shared with it upon request. If members record for the group, at least two should take notes, since group events are complex and at least two ways of perceiving them are essential if the recording is to be at all meaningful.

Audio and video tapes can be profitably employed in various ways, and it is possible to tape every group session. If this step is decided upon, for research or supervision purposes or to enable both leader and members to go over particularly instructive sessions in order to learn more from them, this decision should also be presented during the first meeting as an integral part of the setting. Objections will generally not arise if the tape recorder is permitted for these reasons and the leader assures professional confidentiality. If the agreement is that recording equipment be allowed only when the group opts for it, rather than on a regular basis, the potential benefits of the option should be explained and demonstrated. Tapes ought to be accessible so that interested members can listen to them between sessions, with or without the leader.

Leaders' own notes — preferably jotted down soon after each meeting — are theirs to do with as they see fit. They will undoubtedly refer to these notes during supervision, and the notes may turn out to be their diaries of group life. For most neophytes, note taking immediately after group sessions is a very instructive device. With time and experience leaders gain more confidence, and scrupulous note taking becomes less important.

Although tapes are very helpful, their contribution must not be overrated. Group meetings tend to last an hour and a half; that means a lot of replay time. Technical deficiencies frequently crop up so that not everything can be clearly seen or heard. And, of course, the element of immediacy is bound to be missing.

I find the proper use of the one-way screen a very good recording device. In the observation booth, supervisor, observers, and trainees can watch, record, fill out observation schedules, and exchange views on unfolding group events. In short, they can actively experience the proceedings of the group without in any way disturbing ongoing group life. At its first session, the group should be informed about the one-way screen and its legitimate uses, and assured that only professionals known to the leader will be watching. No more than that is required. Now and again members will refer to the mirror and to what may be taking place behind it. Such references are not necessarily paranoid.

CONFIDENTIALITY

As far as leaders are concerned, group events and member disclosures must be confidential. Leaders may legitimately share them only with professional peers and supervisors. In disguised form, leaders may refer to them with trainees and students and in professional writing. If leaders see certain group members in individual sessions as well, they may, of course, refer in the dyadic interviews to group events pertaining to those members. Except when specifically authorized by the member in question, a leader has no right to impart information regarding occurrences in the group to anyone else. When the leader is convinced that certain data should be communicated to some important figure in the member's environment, he or she should consult with the member in question. Together, they must decide whether the information will be passed on, by whom, and in what manner.

In my experience, however, I have found that the problem of confidentiality lies not with leaders but with participants themselves. Under the best of circumstances, a group decision on this issue, even if easily reached, may be interpreted so differently by group members that the results can prove quite startling. When the problem arises — it may be raised by either leaders or members — leaders can state their own position simply and succinctly. Members find the issue far more complicated. Should they not discuss group events with anyone outside of the group, including group members themselves? Can they refer to group happenings among family and friends without mentioning names or identifying specific participants? Why can't members just trust to the good judgment of everyone and be done with it?

The question of confidentiality does not trouble all groups equally. Patients on the same ward, rehabilitants resident at a center, and, at the other extreme, strangers who are unlikely to meet outside of the group may not even raise the issue. On the other hand, it may deeply concern participants in a work team who meet every workday outside of the group and who interact as well with other members of the system who are not members of the team. In this case the influence of leaders is limited. They can help groups confront the issue and set up their own norms, but they cannot force members to live up to them. What they can do lies in two directions. First, when asked to set up a team composed of members who work together and interact a great deal outside of the projected group, they must point out the inherent problems of confidentiality, emphasize their powerlessness over behavior outside the group, invite reactions, and help the team come to a decision. Second, they can work with their groups primarily on issues directly relevant to the work situation. Beyond that, the group is on its own.

PRE- AND POSTMEETING CONTACTS

If you are in the habit of attending concerts and tend to arrive early, you will undoubtedly have noticed how orchestra members straggle in — singly, in pairs, and small groups. Some head straight for their music stands, while others stand about and chat. As concert time approaches, the pit fills up, instruments are tuned, and last minute remarks exchanged. When the conductor appears, everyone falls silent. The concert is about to begin.

You might wish to compare this picture with how your own

groups tune up. Group meetings get under way before they offi-
cially start, and sometimes end long after the meeting has ostensibly finished. The other day I said in one of my groups, "As far as
I'm concerned, we can get started." A member retorted, "What do
you think has been going on? We have started!" Leaders are not
always aware of — and are often surprised by — the extent of pre-
and postsession contact. Members may meet for a snack or just a
chat before meetings. They may travel together on the same bus or
run into one another in the elevator. If there is a waiting room,
members will frequently gather there. Among other characteristics,
it is easy to identify the loners and the mixers in your group by just
glancing into the waiting room. Some members automatically take
on the role of host, still others that of guest; some arrive compulsively early, others always come late.

When the group finally assembles in its appointed meeting place,
much desultory activity can be observed: chairs are moved, ashtrays
searched for, outer garments removed; people exchange glances and
an occasional smile. And through it all, there is a low hum of con-
versation. Then, all of a sudden, as though by command, the group
falls silent. Everyone now knows that the session has, in fact, begun. The group somehow senses the qualitative difference between
what precedes the meeting, and the meeting itself.

Postmeeting contacts are generally more accessible to the leader's
scrutiny than premeeting contacts, since leaders do not tend to arrive at group meetings much ahead of time. A leader may wish to
linger a moment to exchange remarks or greetings. Participants may
request a word. Looking around, the leader may observe people
leaving alone or in clusters, remaining to continue some unfinished
business, or gathering about a member who was the target of that
particular session. Some people, of course, will be rearranging chairs
and tables. What, if anything, goes on beyond this, leaders may
never know. As far as I am concerned, there is no reason that they
should.

What can leaders do with the pre- and postsession contacts they
do observe? They should take note of them, just as they do of
everything else that occurs in their groups.

Arriving for a meeting, Bill Thomas remarked:

> As I came in just now I noticed some of you listening
> to a tape of one of our meetings. Anything there you
> want us to talk about before we hear Judy's plan?

Joe Smith, who doesn't care for long silences, began a session:
> Hey there, Charlie! I noticed you and Mac playing
> checkers outside before the meeting. How come you
> never find anything to say to each other in here?

Bob Jones once commented to the committee:
> After our last session, I noticed that all of you made
> an unusually quick exit. I wonder if that means any-
> thing about our work together. Would anyone like to
> talk about this?

In Gloria Brown's parents' group, Alice and Louise had clashed
head-on several times concerning permissiveness toward children.
Lately, Gloria had noticed them leaving together. She wondered
aloud about this in the group one day, and discovered that the two
had become good friends, although still disagreeing violently about
child-rearing practices.

When leaders use material from pre- and postsession contacts,
members frequently learn to follow this example. This material is
often relevant to the entire group, not only for the members concerned. It is also a good way of getting closed members to open up:

> As we were leaving last time, Joan made some very
> pertinent comments to me about the group. I told her
> I would ask her to repeat what she told me before all
> of you, and she agreed. So, Joan, how about it?

Leaders should avoid the pitfalls of standoffishness on the one
hand and overinvolvement on the other. They should arrange their
schedules in such a way that they have a few minutes to spare after
each meeting for questions and comments, to listen and to be
listened to, if necessary. Leaders who gather their belongings and
bolt as soon as the session ends will be giving the impression that
their interest in the group is merely within the line of duty, and
that, personally, they couldn't care less about the individual participants. No better are the ones who so identify with the group that
they find it difficult to leave until the very last member has departed.

How should leaders treat personal material furnished them by
individual members between sessions? When appropriate, they
should encourage members to bring up the matter within the group.
Whenever possible leaders should refrain from discussing group or
a specific member's behavior with individual members outside of

group meetings. Approaching the leader may be one way of avoiding the group. If, despite all efforts, members themselves refuse to present the matter to the group, they may still be amenable to the leader's doing so in their stead. An unqualified refusal, however, should be respected.

GROUP TERMINATION

The life of the small groups we are discussing, important, meaningful, and useful as it is for its members, should not be mistaken for life itself. Groups conducted by the helping professions are meant to make life richer, more worthwhile, and easier to cope with. They are by no means substitutes for it. Such groups are not natural occurrences; they are artificially created and must pass away in an artificial manner.

These remarks are intended to prepare you for the realization that the termination of every group should be kept in mind and planned for from the very initiation of group life. At my university, I lead some groups that are scheduled to run once weekly from October to June. Their termination date is known in advance. Nevertheless, I tell students in the fall that spring is just around the corner; in winter I remind them that summer will soon be upon us. Time, I insist, is an important dimension of group life. Members must learn to comprehend this and act accordingly. By keeping group termination in mind, the leader achieves various goals. First, it emphasizes the temporary nature of the group's existence. Second, it tends to discourage overdependence. Third, the leader can remain, and thus help the group to remain, realistic about group goals. In short, timetables enable the group leader and members to see the group in its proper perspective — a transient episode in life, no more, no less.

Aside from therapeutic groups for seriously ill patients — and even here I am not certain that this is always a contraindication — groups work best, I have found, when the number of sessions the group will spend together is known in advance by everyone concerned. This is likely to happen in any case. Groups at schools and universities are generally limited to the academic year. Gloria's parents' group at the child guidance clinic was scheduled, in advance, to run for twenty meetings, a fact that was imparted to candidates when they were interviewed by Gloria. Bill's group, as we have seen, could meet only eight times before rehabilitants were to leave the Center. Joe's group was set up as an open one, so, of course, no time limit could be set. Bob's situation turned out to be somewhat more complicated. Originally, the committee and he had decided on ten weekly sessions. As these were drawing toward their conclusion, Bob pointed this out and suggested that participants plan accordingly. They nodded assent but ignored his suggestion. As the last meeting approached and Bob became more insistent, they proposed disregarding the agreed-upon deadline and continuing to meet. Bob felt he could not accept this, and he, in turn, proposed an evaluation session to assess the work thus far accomplished and that remaining to be done. The group agreed but found "legitimate" reasons for postponing the evaluation session from week to week. In fact, it never took place at all.

However, there is nothing sacred or inviolable about timetables. Here again, flexibility and common sense should prevail. If the group has not finished its work during the time allotted, there is every reason to set a new terminal date if there exists a better than even chance that more time will help, if members and leader agree to the extension, and other basic requirements are secured. My only caution, then, to group and leader alike is this: beware of group addiction!

Sooner or later the day arrives. It has been my experience that at these final sessions, little real learning takes place. The curve, which started low, has risen, and then gradually descended. Members are excited. Addresses and phone numbers are exchanged; promises to keep in touch, to write, to call, to meet, are made. Often the meeting is festively celebrated in a restaurant, or in the regular meeting place with refreshments provided by group members who, sometimes for the first and last time in the group, are complimented, if only for their cakes or sandwiches. Feeble attempts are made at summing up group and individual learnings, and skits presented that poke gentle fun at group and leader alike. The leader is drawn into the fun. The history that is about to come to an end is reviewed, soon to be revised by each member according to his or her own perceptions. Now it is all over; everyone has dispersed. Let us hope the experience has been worthwhile for all concerned.

THE BEHAVIOR OF SMALL GROUPS

In group life, members and leaders behave. Sooner or later, as a result of their actions and interactions, the group will acquire an identity. I do not wish to enter the debate of whether groups take on a personality of their own or even whether such an entity as a "group" exists — the group at times being defined as merely the sum of the behaviors of all its participants. Suffice it to say that members and leaders alike speak of their "group." You will hear, "Our group was awful today. We just never got moving"; or, "Our group was terrific; everyone joined in." Leaders may confide to their colleagues, "I've seen some sluggish groups in my life, but this one beats them all"; or, "I really get a kick out of that Tuesday group. It's always full of action and people don't hold their punches." Clearly, those *of* the group *are* the group. Yet, without resorting to anthropomorphism or appealing to mystique, I believe that goups as such do *behave*. Some seem restless, others tranquil; some are hostile, others friendly; some are very verbal, others much less so; some meet voluntarily, others because they are compelled to. In this section, I shall point out certain aspects of the behaviors of small groups that are worth paying attention to.

1.   Group life has its ups and downs. Changes of mood and behavior can be observed in individual sessions and throughout the development of a group. A certain rhythm can be discerned: passivity after activity; relaxation after tension; horseplay after hard work; expressions of warmth after outbursts of hostility. Ups and downs can be detected in leader behavior as well: relative inaction after intensive interventions; focus on the group after dyadic interactions. Beginning leaders sometimes feel discouraged when their group does not move forward in a straight projection. They become frustrated by the ups and downs and feel it is up to them to smooth these out. In time they will appreciate the fact that group development cannot and, therefore, must not be forced.

The same sort of rhythmic motion is discernible in main and side issues, major and minor themes. Sometimes these are not easily differentiated. At other times they are clearly marked. Frequently, side issues turn out to be main issues in disguise — if the leader can learn to draw upon them at the appropriate moment. Some themes will reappear persistently; perhaps they require further elaboration or different handling. At times, main issues are quickly resolved and never again mentioned. What leaders should do — and this they *must* learn — is to lead their orchestras so sensitively that all themes are heard, though never in cacophony. They can bring side issues to the fore and give major themes a rest, but they must ensure that the entire score gets played.

What is time well spent, as opposed to time wasted by the group? I don't always know. Sometimes I ask the group for its opinion; sometimes I don't. Often, a long-range perspective is needed to evaluate these intangibles. I am at present meeting with a group that for ten sessions persistently returned to the issue of whether it really wanted to go on meeting and working as a team. I was bored and slightly irritated by the endless variations on that theme, and confronted the group with my feelings. I think I understand the concerns expressed and am glad they did not remain hidden. At last the group decided. It took a long time, but was this really time wasted? The future will tell.

2.   Confusion appears in every group, but in some it seems to dominate. People talk all at once and, seemingly, at cross-purposes. They find it hard to listen, to settle on one plan of action. They wish to discuss everything at once. Confusion may remain an essential part of such a group's life or it may begin to dwindle. But even in the most orderly of groups, confusion will occur. It will be encountered at the beginning of meetings, when the group shifts from topic to topic, when something unexpected or dramatic takes place, or simply when the group does not know what to do next. Constant confusion, a criterion often used in this context, may express resistance to the leader, the group, or to both. It may indicate that the group is poorly constituted, the choice of leader an inappropriate one, or, possibly, that its members are not ready for or interested in group life.

Occasional confusion, on the other hand, is easily tolerated by most leaders and can be profitably exploited for group learnings. The leader may help the group analyze the confusion or, alternatively, everyone may ignore it and pass on to the next event in the group's life. **Content** and **process** considerations may be brought up for discussion to ascertain what people were trying to communicate, how they were accomplishing this, and how they felt about the proceedings. **Task** and **maintenance** issues may be raised: Is this a fruitful way to accomplish our task? Do we recall what our task actually is? Did the confusion answer our personal or interpersonal needs? Were we working too hard, or not hard enough? Was everyone involved, or did some feel left out? Should the leader have stepped in more decisively? Are members, perhaps, relying on the leader too much? Is it worthwhile going on now, or should we call it a day?

Bob Jones's committee never knew a moment's confusion. Joe Smith's group experienced a great deal of it. Smith thrived on confusion, as he believed it would eventually force members to break through into some form of order. After the life plan decision, Bill Thomas's group achieved a relative amount of order, confusion tending to prevail toward the end of meetings. Gloria Brown sensed some confusion in her parents' group but was not overly disturbed by it. She noticed that it tended to crop up most conspicuously when the group moved from consideration of one child to another. This seemed to Gloria reasonable enough and her supervisor agreed.

3. Each group tends to emphasize either **cognitive** or **emotional** learnings to a greater degree, and the group leader must at all times be aware of the difference between the two. Joe Smith's group of patients did not care much about the cognitive aspects of personality theory or the causes of pathology. They worried about their inadequacies, anxieties, dreams, and the reality out there. They tried to understand their emotions and express their feelings. When Joe from time to time suggested a book or an article for them to read, they told him he was "full of it." Bob Jones's committee leaned heavily in the cognitive direction — too much so for its own good, Bob thought, and even told them this, but to no avail. They read avidly, drew up numerous reports and charts, discussed points of theory at great length, but never confronted themselves as persons with emotions. They could not express genuine feelings about how they perceived each other interacting in the committee or, in fact, in their day-to-day relationships. They would not face, much less try to resolve, their interpersonal conflicts. These were not unusually serious, but enough so that, unresolved, their organization development program never got off the ground.

4. The group may exert pressure — both on the leader and on the various members in the group. Although Gloria knew about

group pressure from books and lectures, even more from her experience in groups as both member and observer, she was completely taken aback when she realized that she did not know how to handle her parents' group's pressure upon her for the answer to a specific problem. Gloria was well aware that she did not possess the answer, and that even if she thought she did, it might not be a meaningful one for the group or be understood as she intended. She did not wish to be obstinate and wanted the group to like her. She also wanted members to get something out of the group. She even feared, at times, that the group might disintegrate if she were to resist group pressure too strongly, and that her nightmare might be actualized. She and her supervisor worked long and hard on this problem.

Group pressure can be cruel. It may be exerted on a member perceived by the majority as someone who thinks and behaves deviantly, on closely knit subgroups that refuse to bow to group norms, on representatives of ethnic or religious minorities who are viewed stereotypically and not as the individuals they are, as well as on the leaders themselves. Leaders find it much easier to protect individual members from group pressure than to stand up to it when it is directed against themselves. Groups seek solutions to their problems, answers to their questions. That is, after all, the reason they come together in the first place. They expect the leader to provide the solutions. After all, the leader openly defines him- or herself as the person leading the group. If the leader doesn't know or won't tell or keeps beating around the bush, why bother. It would be better to look for another group, another leader, or another tranquilizer.

When and if this issue arises, it is best to confront it head on. Leaders ought to reflect their groups' feelings empathically and express their own clearly and decisively. To some problems there is no solution. Solutions are interpreted in different ways by different people. Meaningful answers exist only to specific questions in specifically defined and understood situations. Solutions and answers do not help but only serve to confuse and frustrate if they cannot be carried out. Sometimes solutions become irrelevant when we can change or, at least, understand better certain of our behaviors. Answers may seem less important when one realizes that everyone in the group has to learn to deal with situations to which there can be no answer except for that arrived at through trial and error, patience and determination.

The group setting exists because leaders truly believe that members can learn from one another when they can begin to listen, trust one another, and stop regarding the leader as the fount of all knowledge. For their part, leaders are prepared to do their share when they feel certain they have a contribution to make that will be meaningful to their groups. Leaders are open to questions at all times, but will not yield to group pressure when they perceive it as unjustified.

5.   When all is said and done, some groups tend to be more dependent than others, some flaunt their counterdependence, while still others follow a consistently independent course. Bill's group — once it had discovered, with his help, a way of proceeding — functioned quite independently. Bob's, on the other hand, in spite of everything he tried — including sharing his perceptions of their behavior — remained counterdependent to the bitter end. Members always found legitimate reasons for turning down his suggestions and for not confronting the interpersonal issues within the committee. They continued calling him "Professor," and were deferential to the last moment.

Joe Smith isn't completely satisfied with his groups unless they express a great deal of hostility and aggression. He believes that these legitimate feelings are usually just below the surface anyway, and can be dealt with effectively only when brought out into the open. However, after a tense "fight" session, he anticipates joking, a more relaxed atmosphere, and "flight" behavior (Bion, 1961). He encourages fight, as indicated, but feels pretty comfortable with flight as well. He has learned that the one is impossible without the other.

6.   All groups require warmth and protection — some more and some less. These cannot be artificially produced and seem to be a function of the leader's personality, style, and behavior in the group. It is worth noting that too much warmth may produce torpor and too much protection stultify growth. Although Joe Smith had no need to protect members from attack, believing as he did that they had to learn to fend for themselves, his warm personality and obvious caring did much to generate a feeling of belonging and sharing.

7.   Although groups, like individuals, respond to the expectations of their leader (Frank, 1961), some are more oriented toward

feelings, while others tend toward the cognitive. Whichever the case, leaders must help their groups achieve their goals, and that may involve, at times, stressing just those aspects that seem to them neglected. Some groups are simply more active than others. Experienced leaders, whose style has crystallized over the years, will attest to this. Passive groups demand more leader interventions while active ones often require harder concentration. Similarly, some groups are better talkers and others better listeners. For the new leader, it is obvious, the verbal group is easier to manage, but if it cannot develop listening skills as well it won't get very far. It goes without saying that listeners make an excellent audience only when there are talkers available.

As will be seen in more detail in the chapters that follow, some groups stress and examine their own dynamics, while others play up interpersonal and even intrapersonal concerns. Some delve into control, power, and leadership issues whereas others deal much more with affiliation and affection needs. The emphasis will depend somewhat on group goals and on leader style, but it is also a function of the group as such.

Before concluding the present chapter, I should like to share one of my own rather late learnings: not all groups learn. This may be due to their composition, the shortcomings of their leader, or the imponderables of the learning process. It might be due to the fact that not all people are able to learn in groups, and when this type predominates, the group will be stymied. Some people learn better in dyads, some do best alone with a little guidance. Some, I fear, will not learn under any circumstances.

5
Member Skills

PROCESS SKILLS

In this and the following chapter, I wish to discuss some of the skills needed by group members and the group leader to promote effective learning. The professional worker in the dyadic relationship is already familiar with many of these skills, and I shall, therefore, dwell at greater length only on those that relate more specifically to work with groups. The present chapter will deal with the skills of members, while the next will be devoted to those of the group leader. Since many of the skills pertain to the behavior of member and leader alike, this division is somewhat artificial and is attempted here merely for didactic purposes. I begin with the process skills of members.

Process skills are those particular behaviors with which the group member becomes familiar through practice and repeated use in the group. These enable him or her to react and respond adequately to the way group matters are dealt with and integrated in the group. These skills depend less on what is being said and more on *how* it is being said and how it affects speaker and listeners; how members treat each other's feelings, ideas, and perceptions; how people are included or excluded; how group or individual problems are chosen, handled, and decided; under what conditions members learn best.

These process skills — once practiced, learned, and interjected — facilitate the work of the group. They enhance group communication on the one hand and promote individual and group learnings on the other, providing a climate wherein members feel cared for, respected, trusted, and yet confronted and challenged directly by the interested listening, observing, and evaluating of the group — all of this so that learning can take place and behavioral changes can be weighed and attempted. Groups, of course, function at very different levels of process involvement. Some group leaders focus mainly on content, whereas others prefer process issues. Process skills come to be particularly esteemed in those groups in which genuine interaction takes place because members have learned that these skills can contribute to their learnings.

The skills I am about to discuss are acquired in various ways. Some members bring them into the group; although they have never consciously used these skills, the members are just good, natural processors able, for example, to listen intensely. Most of us need to become more aware of and to practice process skills. Some leaders prefer working on these as part of the development of the group, and others utilize specific exercises stressing specific skills. Most of us, I find, members and leaders alike, never become really proficient in taking full advantage of our process skills. Therefore, every group member can help us to sharpen these tools and to become more aware of those occasions when we are remiss because of our momentary overinvolvement, inattention, or other human failings.

The four skills I wish to discuss at this point seem to me the most facilitating, on the one hand, and, on the other, the most difficult to apply productively. By far the most important of these is **listening.** Despite all that has been said and written on this by now rather hackneyed subject, we remain poor listeners. This shortcoming may be inherent in some of us or, perhaps, it is culturally induced. Whatever the reason, I continue to be astounded by the lack of sensitive listening in groups. We often find it difficult or impossible to repeat or even to summarize accurately what has just been said. We were preoccupied with our own thoughts; we were busy preparing a reply; we knew, or thought we knew, what was going to be said and stopped paying attention; we were distracted by something happening within us or in the group; we were put off by the manner in which things were being said. Whatever the reasons, the fact remains that we did not or could not or would not listen.

If we recognize the shortcoming as ours, it can be rectified somewhat by our telling the speaker frankly that we were not listening and by asking him or her to repeat. If we sense the shortcoming lies in the speaker's rambling sentences, florid style, or unnecessary repetitions, we may be faced with a dilemma. On the one hand, we know we did not listen and, therefore, could not have understood. On the other, it is the speaker who has put us into this uncomfortable position because of his or her way of speaking, and we may not be prepared to pay the price of understanding. It takes an effort for me to face Charlie and tell him straight out why I can't listen to him. He may feel hurt. Perhaps he can't talk any other way. Why should I risk incurring his displeasure or even hostility? The result may be that Charlie will never know that I don't listen to him, and why this is so.

Let us now assume that we were listening, that we can repeat what has been said. What did we hear, what did we listen for? When Ruth, in Gloria Brown's group, told of her broken marriage, Gladys listened to every word. She thought of her own marriage and of all the compromises she was making and would go on making just to keep it going. When she heard of the trouble Ruth was having in raising her kids, her own troubles seemed to dwindle. She wouldn't want to be in Ruth's shoes under any circumstances. But could Gladys really try on Ruth's shoes for size, try to feel what it would be like to be Ruth?

Only when Gloria responded to Ruth's outpourings did Gladys suddenly realize that she had not understood, that she had listened but had not heard what was there below the surface of the words. There was Gloria (and even Alice and Louise were exchanging glances of approval) telling Ruth that she heard strength, determination, and joy in Ruth's story. Gloria had understood Ruth to say that she was kind of proud of herself for having left her husband; that, with all the hardships, it was easier and better now, and that she, Ruth, now hoped to become less dependent and more mature. Gladys hadn't heard any of these emotional undertones. She was very glad she had not spoken up immediately to tell Ruth she ought to go back to her husband for the children's sake, at least. And now, here was Sylvia telling Ruth she admired her guts, and suggesting that she need not spoil the kids just because their father was gone. Weeks later when Ruth again spoke, Gladys still did not agree with her, but this time she listened better and heard more. She heard anxiety and fear and frustration. Suddenly she heard herself saying:

> Last time you spoke and people reacted, I didn't know what was going on. I kept saying to myself that you were all wrong and that I wouldn't trade places with you for anything. Today I still think that I, in your place, would have kept that marriage going, but I

think I understand you better. You don't sound so
brave and sure of yourself to me, but you're really
honest and I respect you for that. I wish I could be
that honest with myself.

Andrew, in Joe Smith's therapy group, listened best with his eyes.
He would say things like "You sound sad but you look damned
pleased with yourself"; or, "Your words are so calm and bland —
why do you look as if you would like to kill us?" Some of Bill
Thomas's blind rehabilitants picked up all kinds of cues in the
group. Once Helen said to Clark:

Your life plan sounds just terrific; everyone is going
to help you and welcome you and never mind that
you're blind so long as you can do the job like anyone
else. And you sound as if you really believe it. But if
you're so sure, why are you so nervous? You keep
scraping your shoes and you clear your throat after
every sentence. You'd better wake up from your
dreaming, my boy, before you get too many knocks
out there.

When Joe Smith noticed that Charlie's way of talking was increasingly rubbing people the wrong way, and that he himself had
to work hard to pay attention, he decided one evening to put Charlie
straight. In the literature, this is called **confrontation.** Here is what
he said:

There you go again, Charlie. Long complicated sentences, fancy talk, and over and over again the same
stuff! It's hard for me to listen to you and as I look
around, I see I'm not the only one. Now we know why
you talk like that; you know and we know that you're
scared to talk and you're scared to breathe and you're
scared to shit. But if you want us to listen to you, talk
simply, talk to the point. Why haven't some of you
people told Charlie how his talking affects you? We
aren't being really fair to him this way.

Charlie left the session feeling very hurt, but from then on at least
he was aware of how he came across, and he made an effort to
change. No miracle occurred, but in consequence of the confrontation, group members tried harder to listen; Charlie lost some of his
fear, too.

Sensitive listening and sharing with others what I have heard them say, what their words have made me feel, and what reactions they evoke in me, is a form of feedback. Confrontation is another form, hard to give and hard to accept. It is a kind of summing up of the impact others make on me and a statement of how I want to see them behave, so that it will be easier for me to get closer to them, understand them more fully, like them better. It is direct, personal, and evaluative, and it is meant to be so. It says, without mincing words: this is what your behavior does to me. If you intend something else, then you are not achieving your goal, you will have to change your behavior, and, if you wish to reach me, the direction is . . .

Both Joe Smith and Bob Jones knew themselves to be very confronting. In his therapy group, Joe's confrontations were, ultimately, accepted. Bob met with much less success with the committee. The committee as a group and its members as individuals responded well to his confrontations — too well, he thought. They agreed with him, admired his perspicacity, implied they would try to change. At one point in an early meeting, Bob said:

> You people say you want to improve your interpersonal communication, but whenever something along that line comes up, you shy away from it as if it were poison. Right now, for example, you, Ted, if I heard you correctly, were telling Sam that he often says one thing but really behaves as if he believed something quite different. Just then you, Pete, stepped in to say that Ted and Sam should work that out some other time, and that the committee'd better decide what to do about your report.

The report was dutifully laid aside, and Ted and Sam tried to communicate. As a result, Sam became defensive, Ted apologetic, and Pete annoyed. Bob confronted them with this as well, but by that time they had to quit.

Feedback is a skill that group members use when they are ready to share their perceptions of another member with him or her. They assume that these perceptions, nonthreateningly offered, may help the other learn how he or she comes across. The receiver of the feedback may ignore the data, think it over, or request more, wishing perhaps to hear from other members as well. Feedback is a good skill with which to point out aspects of our behavior to which we may be oblivious — to uncurtain one of the panes of the Johari window. I shall refer to it again when discussing leader skills. Here I wish to allude to those criteria involved in the giving of feedback that may help members judge whether the feedback presented was skillfully offered, so that the receiver, assuming openness on his or her part, could easily grasp it.

Understanding feedback is not primarily a cognitive difficulty; on the contrary, it is emotional. To hear something concerning myself about which I may be totally unaware — and from a relative stranger, at that — demands on my part a readiness to listen, and on the giver's part, a way of presenting the feedback so that I will not feel threatened enough to set up defenses, thus preventing the message from reaching me as it was intended.

As I see it, the least threatening feedback meets all or at least most of the following criteria:

1.   It is descriptive rather than evaluative.

2.   It is as close and immediate as possible to the set of behaviors that elicited the feedback.

3.   It must be well timed, in the sense of being offered when, hopefully, the recipient is emotionally ready to hear it.

4.   It should be presented not to settle scores with the recipient, but because the giver feels it can be useful.

5.   It should, if not directly solicited, at least not be imposed upon the receiver.

6.   It should be checked out to insure that it was correctly understood.

The last process skill I want to touch upon is the most difficult of all to put into practice — that of **giving and receiving help.** This is essentially a matter of attitude, not of technique. Although individuals participate in groups because, in one way or another, they are seeking help, it is not easy for them to admit this to themselves, let alone to others. The matter becomes more delicate still when their participation in the group is not entirely voluntary. If they are ready to face the fact that they need help, they demand it at first from the leader of the group, certainly not from other group members who have come for the same purpose. It may take quite some time until they realize that all members are not in need of identical help, although they know cognitively that everyone's problems are different. But suddenly a group member will make a point that strikes home; the leader could not have put it more aptly. A particular group member will seem to understand another member better than anyone else, including the leader. Something will happen in the group that stirs that other person into a readiness to share some of the hidden thoughts and feelings that he or she was certain could never be expressed anywhere.

The most exciting thing of all happens when participants suddenly realize one day that they, ordinary group members, can help, that they are actually helping other participants in the group. They really haven't done very much; they merely stated what they thought, expressed what they felt, tendered feedback because it had been requested. When group members can clearly see that their words have made an impact, they feel elated and proud.

In the parents' group, Gladys countered:
> Gloria, you didn't get the point. Ruth and Louise did. What I meant to say is that my husband isn't forcing me to behave that way. It is me who is forcing myself because I think that's what he wants . . . and then I blame him for forcing me. Ruth's husband really did force her, but mine is a weakling. I suppose I so want him to be strong that I act as if he were.

A few sessions after Joe Smith had confronted Charlie, the latter told the group:
> Sure, I didn't like what Joe said. I was stunned. But when some of you fellows agreed with him, that really got me thinking. And when after the meeting some of you stuck around just to chat, I began to feel better. Now I'm glad you said it, Joe, but if you others had kept your mouths shut then, I'd still be mad.

There are many occasions when group members will accept from another participant what they would surely reject had it come from the leader, although it is true that for others the leader remains central throughout group life. What really matters, I think, is that if group participants can learn to listen well, confront directly but not viciously, and give nonthreatening feedback, they will be able to help others much more than they could have believed possible. Moreover, these skills serve them well outside of the group, too. True, not everyone can take confrontation or invite feedback, but most people do like and do need to be listened to.

THE NEED TO BE LISTENED TO
AND UNDERSTOOD

This need to be listened to and understood seems to be universal among people today. I would venture the guess that were people to ask themselves frankly why they join groups of one kind or another, the most frequent answer would be to fulfill that need. As will be recalled, Bill Thomas's group was not set up on a voluntary basis, and it had a hard time getting started. It functioned well because of the technique of the life-plan idea, but when Bill asked participants before their discharge from the Center whether they would recommend this type of group for other rehabilitants, he was surprised to find that everyone answered in the affirmative. After a little probing, they all agreed that what had meant most to them in the group had been the opportunity to be listened to and understood. This seemed a little strange to Bill. After all, they had been living together at the Center for months, and had, in fact, expressed their initial opposition to the group in terms of this. And then Bill experienced one of the most rewarding moments of his life. The rehabilitants told him that it was he who had really listened to and understood them, and, by so doing, had enabled them, after months of talking *at* each other, to listen and understand as well. They added that the sighted rarely understand the blind — perhaps because excessive pity gets in the way. At first the group had resented Bill's nonchalant manner; they had mistaken it for indifference. They now knew better; that was his veneer, but underneath they found him deeply interested and caring and, what they appreciated most, not exaggeratedly optimistic about the plans they had presented.

Once Bob Jones, in one of his counseling groups, noticed a member mumbling under her breath. She turned to her neighbor and whispered to him. After a while, Bob asked her if she was prepared to say something to the group. This helped her get started. All of us in the field of group work have seen silent members begin to talk, hesitate, and withdraw as the talkers, not even having noticed the usually silent members, take over once again. Only after a bit of prodding on the part of the leader will the silent ones admit that they really meant to speak up, more often than not adding hastily that their contributions were of no consequence anyway. The talkers are generally taken aback by such an interchange, not having realized previously that the silent ones are often silent because the others do not listen.

Before leaving this topic, I shall permit myself a bit of advice to my neophyte reader: whatever you do, do not get in the way, do not prevent people from being listened to and understood. This warning may, perhaps, sound silly or even offensive, for it is not easy to see oneself as behaving this way. But I have seen so many beginning group leaders stumble right here that I permit myself the warning. There is so much to watch out for in the group and in ourselves that at times we do, unintentionally, get in the way. Let one example suffice to illustrate what I mean. I once observed a new, very competent leader working with a group of educators. They did not exactly understand what she meant when she encouraged them to interact in an open manner and to express feelings. In her opinion they were remaining closed and uptight. At one point in the proceedings, she suggested that people tell in a few words what was bothering them most as educators. The dam burst: the need to be listened to had been aroused but — you have guessed it — she insisted that they limit themselves to a brief statement. The opportunity had come and she had muffed it. Luckily for all, the group's need proved stronger than the leader's direction.

SOCIOMETRIC ASSESSMENT

Another skill I like to develop among group members is **sociometric assessment:** the stating of social preferences within the group, backed up by subjective reasons for the choices made. Sociometric assessment was originated by Moreno (1953), and further refined by some of his disciples (Northway, 1967; Lindzey and Byrne, 1969). I know that some will take issue with me, and maintain that sociometric assessment stresses evaluation rather than description, hierarchy rather than equality. The skill must be employed discriminatingly, I agree, but I am certain that evaluation need not always be negative and that hierarchy in groups exists and should not be entirely ignored.

This year I am working with a group that finds it difficult to get started. All its members chose the group voluntarily and attend sessions faithfully. It is just not a very verbal group. The other day, to help them over the initial hurdle, I gave them the following direction, "Tell us who, in your opinion, contributes most to this group and how. What in his or her behavior would you like to be able to imitate? Then, if you wish, tell us who is the member who has, so far, contributed least, and what in his or her behavior you would not like to imitate." The reaction was dumbfounded silence. I added that the group was, of course, free to disregard my suggestion. Hesitantly at first, they accepted the challenge. This group session turned out to be one of the finest it has been my pleasure to witness in a long time. Member contributions were variously perceived. Candidates were suggested from many different frames of reference. Some members learned for the first time that they were seen as contributing, and in just what way. Others learned that their intentions had been misunderstood by some participants and ignored by others. One member who was widely praised for her successful contributions became terribly upset: she feared success as it demanded more of her than she felt she had to give.

I like to employ sociometric assessment as a form of feedback. When I ask a group of teachers in an in-service training program to choose from among themselves who they would like as their teacher, giving a specific reason for their choice, as well as who they would not want, again giving a reason, a great deal of information is generated. If the reasons given for choosing or rejecting one are clear and specific, members can learn a lot about their behavior as perceived by others. This skill cannot be attempted with every group, and should not, of course, be practiced until a group has learned to give and to receive feedback.

A group of kindergarten teachers met once a week for the purpose of improving their communication skills with parents and children. After we were well acquainted with each other and the group had become cohesive, I suggested the following exercise. "If, from tomorrow morning on, you had to work in pairs in your kindergarten, and had to pick from this group the partner who would understand you best and yet would not let you dominate her, whom would you choose and why? Be as specific as you can." The teachers learned a great deal during that session about how others see them.

Sociometric assessment almost backfired on me once. I was conducting a workshop of Israeli Jewish and Arab students who had worked in mixed teams on a joint educational project in Arab villages during the previous summer. They had gathered to sum up their experiences and make plans for a new project (Benjamin, 1972). At one stage of the workshop I asked each member, if given the opportunity to pick a work team of three from among the participants, who would be the choices? Everyone chose, but then they turned to me and demanded that I pick a team as well. I felt, somehow, that I was being challenged; that in a way my personal authenticity was in question. I decided, therefore, not to retreat behind my leader role. I chose my three team members, and told the group what had influenced my choice, and what I knew about my own needs, strengths, and weaknesses that would make this team a successful one, in my opinion. I usually do not comply with such provocations, but am glad I did this once.

The literature is replete with further examples for those interested. My purpose, when concentrating on this skill, is always to stress description and specificity, and to point out the fact that we are all constituted differently, perceive differently, and thus have individual preferences. I try to get as many members as possible involved, and I add only those personal perceptions that I can relate to specific behaviors that have cropped up during the life of the group. I do not find this skill harmful to the group when used with the provisos indicated above.

ROLE-PLAY

Role-play is a member skill that is widely accepted and practiced. It consists of cutting short a participant who is relating an incident involving a relationship with a significant person in his or her life, and suggesting that, instead, it be acted out. The suggestion generally comes first from the leader. Eventually, members may initiate role-play as well. The application and refinement of the skill depend largely on the group's willingness to play-act. Thus some groups never role-play. The attitude of the individual leader is also an important factor. Some leaders are insufficiently familiar with the skill and feel insecure in its use. Others simply discount its efficacy.

Role-play is a technique that demands of the member involved: stop talking about it and live it. Choose someone in the group who looks like or reminds you of, or can just stand for, X. Ask the member if he or she is prepared to be X for a few minutes, and begin role-playing. During the play, the rest of the group observes in silence and does not interfere with the action. The play ends when the actors quit or when the leader or a member suggests cutting. Then the interaction just witnessed is discussed and analyzed, the performers being given priority.

The purpose of this dramatic presentation is to move from words to action, from description and theorizing to actual behavior (Moreno, 1953; Maier et al., 1967). The group member in question usually acts that role while another member tries to behave like the second partner in the relationship. Although that member does not know the person he or she is impersonating, and the little that is known about the part comes from the subjective report of the member involved, role-play can be close enough to reality to invoke behaviors that show far more than mere verbalizing ever could.

Gloria Brown enjoys acting and the theater, and thus it is not surprising that her work in groups leans heavily on role-play. One day, in the parents' group, Gladys spoke at length about the quarrel she and her husband George had had the night before about the upbringing of their five-year-old Tommy. Tommy is an adopted child and knows this. Of late, easygoing Tommy has become rebellious, insisting that his "real mommy" would let him stay up late to watch TV. Gloria stopped Gladys in the midst of her description and asked her to choose someone who would portray George; together they would act out the previous night's argument. Gladys chose Fred, and they acted the scene this way:

> *Gladys*
> I know he's taking advantage of my feelings, but it's easy enough for you to talk. It's never his "real daddy" but only his "real mommy" who would let him have more ice cream or buy him this or that, or would not put him to bed. And then, after a day like

that, you come home all smiles and Tommy can do no wrong and everything is my fault. Now, you go in there and get him away from the TV and into bed. If I do it there's bound to be a ruckus — and why should I always be the bad one?

Fred as George
Oh, let him watch the end of that show. He's really a good kid and you're kinda hard on him lately.

Gladys (crying)
I'm hard on him! Just listen to that. Did it ever occur to you that he might be hard on me? Did it ever occur to you that if not for him I might have. . . . No, I don't really mean that but . . . well, you promised to help bring him up and all you do is spoil and spoil him because you feel sorry for him.

Fred as George
I don't feel sorry for him, though it must be real tough for him.

Gladys (in hysterics)
How about me? Don't I count for anything in this house? If it weren't for you we might have . . .

(Gloria directs them to cut.)

The above scene requires no elaboration. Suffice it to say that during Gladys's recounting of the argument, her deep resentment of her husband's infertility and her thwarted professional ambitions hardly surfaced and did not come across to the group as they did in the play. The rest of the meeting was devoted to Gladys. At one point, a group member proposed role reversal: Gladys would act George and Fred would be Gladys. This time another aspect of her conflict emerged — her role as the only child of parents who had never really wanted children.

Joe Smith prefers that his patients act solo. He likes to use the "empty chair," a technique developed by Fritz Perls (1969). When it became clear to Joe that Charlie was full of repressed aggression toward his father, he suggested at one session that Charlie converse with his father as if he were sitting in the empty chair that Joe had placed opposite him. After a while, Joe suggested that Charlie reverse roles, exchanging chairs as well. The session was a powerful and productive one, as a result of which other members found it easier to examine relations with their own parental figures.

MEMBER ROLES AND BEHAVIORS

In group life as in life generally, members behave and in doing so fill one or several roles. These roles and behaviors may be restricted by the group to such an extent that it becomes impossible for the individual member to break loose. Alternatively, the group may encourage members to play a wide variety of roles and enlarge the scope of their behaviors. Behavior in the group is also a function of the member's own personality and is influenced as well by that of the leader.

As a consequence, we must be wary lest we allow ourselves to generalize from the behavior of members in the group to their behavior in society at large. Group life is restricted and artificial and is not necessarily representative of outside behavior. To some, the group provides a haven and refuge in which they may permit themselves behaviors they would not dare engage in beyond its protective boundaries. To others the contrary is true: it seems confining and frustrating. To others still, the group is an exhilarating, liberating, challenging milieu. All of these persons may transfer their learnings to the outside world with differing degrees of success. Hence the danger in generalization.

Group life affects people very differently and leads to differing degrees of involvement. Some are drawn into it deeply, and, while it lasts and sometimes even beyond that, it becomes the focus of their concerns. Others can take the group or leave it. They barely become involved in it emotionally and tend to remain on the sidelines of group action. Some members become aware of the group only when it actually meets, but participate fully in it then. Others are so awed by the group that it totally paralyzes them. In brief, members' behavior in the small group is not always a good predictor of their behavior or performance outside it.

A few years ago, a nurse participated in one of my groups. This woman, to the best of my recollection, barely opened her mouth during the entire course of the group. I ran into her some time later and found her very active and verbal. When I reminded her of her behavior in the group, she told me that her recollections differed slightly from mine, but commented that at the time she had felt little need to talk and had decided simply to observe others in the group. I also recall a man who was very much liked, and, indeed, was voted one of the most popular members of his group. I learned later that at his plant he is considered difficult to get along with and is heartily disliked. Another example is a young couple who once came to me for therapy. I had known the wife in a group in which she had seemed understanding and active. However, when confronting and confronted by her husband, she appeared an entirely different person.

The contrasting behaviors described above need not be rationalized away; they can rather easily be explained. If, then, behavior is not always transferred or transferable, what are we to make of member behaviors in groups? The answer can be formulated rather neatly, at least on paper. Applying it is far from simple.

As a first step, we can help to create a climate in which no member behavior or role is taken for granted. In other words, all actions are challenged by leader and members alike in order that all members can become more conscious of their behavior, decide how they feel about it, and, if they choose to do so, can try to change it. We are not always fully aware of our behavior and its effects upon others; we are not always conscious of the roles we play or of their impact on the group. When members focus on group behavior and member roles, they may be learning and teaching the ultimate of what the group has to offer.

Must it always be Harry who initiates the discussion? What does this show about him, about the group? Does Harry really want this state of affairs to continue? How does he behave outside the group? What about John, who never initiates discussion? Who in the group offers opinions, comments, suggestions? What about the others? Why do Bruce's suggestions tend to be rejected? Does he perhaps intend them to be? Could he phrase them differently, more forcefully? Will he stop making suggestions after so much criticism? Whose ideas would be more acceptable to the group?

How about Ernie, who can always describe afterwards what has occurred in the group, but who does little to make things happen? Does everyone see him in the role of historian? Does he, himself?

And Irene, who always tries to get everyone to be pals and avoid clashes — what does that show about her? What is she afraid of? How about Lee, always coming up with compromises — is he headed for politics? And Kathy, who always volunteers to be the observer — is that good for her, for the group? What does observing mean for Kathy? What does participation imply for her?

We all laugh at Jack's witticisms. Why is he always joking? Are we somehow telling him that that's all we expect from him? Might he, perhaps, want to be serious? Can Carol express only aggression? Is there nothing else inside? As for Pat, must he at all times follow the leader of the moment? And Sally, can't she let anyone get a word in edgewise? Must she always monopolize? Do we really want to hear Hal constantly baring his soul? Can he speak of nothing else? And how about the silent member? He or she deserves our special attention.

SILENCE

In order to provide some structure to this discussion, I should like to point out that not all silence is resistance and that talk may actually be a mask for avoidance. At times members do not know when or how to say what they might say if they were more confident. On the other hand, we have all come across people who will speak in order not to say anything, to keep others from saying something they would rather remained unsaid, or else to prevent silence from occurring. Silence can, of course, indicate resistance, and talk may be meaningful, but simplistic psychologizing must be avoided, and perceptions should always be checked out.

Let us first consider group silence. As a rule, it should not be encouraged, and during early group sessions not be allowed to get out of hand. Silence has a tendency to feed on itself. If not broken in good time, it may take on proportions no one intended, and nonexistent meanings be sought for it. Groups are often silent because they are waiting for direction. They are silent because they do not know how to proceed, because every member is waiting for someone else to start. Frequently, the smallest push from the leader suffices. "Who is ready to begin today?" or "Let's see, where did we stop last time?" or "As I recall it, Betty, you're going to lead off today — O.K., Betty?" Incidentally, when leader and group decide on having a particular member open each session, as in Bill's group, it is advisable to have a standby prepared in case the scheduled member is absent.

During early sessions in particular, leaders may have to push a little harder. On the other hand, they must watch their behavior carefully, for if their groups become accustomed to their opening each time, that is probably what will continue to happen. If leaders intend that their groups should gradually take over, they should make this clear by acting accordingly from the very beginning of the session.

Silence that occurs during a session can be handled quite differently, since an event has certainly preceded it and may have ostensibly caused it. The best way to find out is to ask. If the leader has some ideas and feelings regarding the silence, he or she may wish to share these with the group. Bill Thomas once broke the silence following Rod's presentation of his life plan by asking:

> What can be causing this silence? Anyone have an idea? [silence] . . . Well, I'll tell you what I think. I think people just don't know what to say or ask, since Rod has told us that he is planning to become a farmhand, and there just don't happen to be any other farmers in this group. Now I happen to have been brought up on a farm, and I'd like to know, Rod, if . . .

When Joe Smith's group ran into a protracted silence, on the other hand, he would generally not bother about interpretations, but would simply turn to a member and ask him or her any question that came to mind.

At times, groups fall silent because they have completed their immediate task, and do not know what to turn to next. But there are other silences that are charged with tension. How to handle these is a matter of leader style and is influenced by group goals. Leaders may decide to break the tension or wait for it to boil over. Hopefully, they will be guided by group needs and not by their own anxieties.

After Gloria had cut the role-play between Gladys and Fred, the group fell silent. Only Gladys's sobs could be heard. The silence continued. Gloria decided to wait it out. Gladys dried her eyes and straightened up. More silence. Finally, Gloria inquired about the meaning of the silence. The group exploded. Some members felt Gloria had been unnecessarily cruel in initiating the play and then letting it go on so long. Others felt compassion for Gladys but had been reluctant to break the silence. Others identified with her husband, George. The group was back at work, no longer silent.

We have not yet dealt with the silent member. I learned an unexpected lesson from Ed, who remained silent session after session. One day, someone turned to him and asked, "Hey, Ed, how come you never say anything?" Ed replied, "Well, no one ever asks me anything, so I just listen to what's going on." This simply shows that there are members who, unless directly engaged, will wait in silence. Others will remain silent because they are afraid of interrupting, or will fall silent because they have been cut off. Some members need only a minimal amount of encouragement to get them started. There are talkers and listeners, active and passive members in every group. If a determined effort is made by active members to bring the more passive ones into the group's interaction, they will be encouraged, eventually, to participate.

Simple encouragement will not always do the trick, however. Some members are inherently inhibited, fearful, hesitant, shy. Some of these can be helped in dyadic therapy. Others will come out of their shells very gradually within the group. Still others will remain silent no matter what is attempted. It has been my experience that certain sensitive group members can get really silent ones involved with much more success than the leader. The element of peer interest seems, at times, to work wonders. Leaders must face the fact that on occasion they can do no more than show silent members that they care about them and are ready to hear what they have to say. But in the final analysis, leaders must respect silence, too. It helps to realize that, in regard to learning in the group, the silent ones may not come off too badly. Their contributions may be minimal, but their presence is strongly felt.

6
Leader Skills

PERCEPTIONS AND FEEDBACK

The skills of leaders and members not only overlap frequently but, to a great degree, depend on and are affected by one another. This interdependence of member and leader behaviors makes it somewhat difficult to analyze them separately, but it is often a factor in the attraction of leaders to group work. Of course, there is a basic difference: the group is, in a very definite sense, under the leader's influence and control. It has come together for the purpose of learning, and it is the leader's task to make this possible. This does not mean that leaders cannot learn in the groups they lead; what it does mean is that the leader's needs and learnings must be subordinated to those of the members. If leaders cannot give priority to their groups cognitively, emotionally, and behaviorally, they should not be leading them. If leaders must demonstrate their knowledge and express their feelings without due regard for the learnings and needs of the group, they are obviously not yet ready to lead. Should this state of affairs persist, it is evident that they have chosen the wrong professional area in which to function.

Leaders do, without doubt, learn from group members. They learn by witnessing their struggles toward a more mature and fuller life. Leaders learn about their shortcomings from the way members relate to them and share with them their perceptions of leader behavior. They learn as well by observing themselves working in groups. But leaders must satisfy in groups only those needs that coincide with or complement those of the particular group.

Group leaders are, first and foremost, teachers. Their teachings are, however, of a special nature. Unlike those contained in books and lectures, their teachings involve their own behaviors, and consequently they must always take these into account. Leadership style, the composite of a leader's behaviors in the group, determines to a great extent how the group will develop and function. An analogy can again effectively be drawn with an orchestra: fine musicians remain so in spite of a mediocre conductor; with a superior one they can achieve great heights of musicianship. Mediocre musicians require an especially competent conductor to mold them into the best orchestra they can become. Group leaders are behavior molders. Ideally, they do not want members to imitate them. They do want to behave in a manner that will enable the members to mold their behaviors according to their own choices and propensities, a goal achieved by consistently demonstrating ways and means whereby behavior can be examined, evaluated, and modified. This demands certain skills, which we shall discuss in this chapter.

Group life generates manifold perceptions. How these are produced, distorted, readjusted, and stabilized, and how ensuing changes are brought about, should become major concerns for the group. The leader's skill in making this endeavor a productive one is essential. What I perceive or do not perceive in the group right now is based, in great part, on my own past experience, which affects my interpretations of what is happening at any given moment. Unless I learn to check out my present perceptions, I cannot know what others in the group are perceiving and to what extent their perceptions are in accord with mine. If I perceive Gloria being cruel to Gladys, I may conclude that Gloria is, in fact, cruel. When that perception is checked out in the group, and I hear from Gladys herself that Gloria was not being cruel, I will have to reassess my perception. If, however, most other members agree with me, I may wonder whether Gladys enjoys being hurt or is, perhaps, covering up for Gloria. Should I be told by someone in the group that whether or not Gloria was being cruel to Gladys is less significant than the fact that I always see people as attacking or hurting others, even when those others do not perceive it that way at all, I can avail myself of the opportunity to receive additional feedback from the group and with its help begin to readjust my perceptions. I do not mean to imply that there are right or wrong perceptions, or that there exists only one way to perceive events. My point is that only when perceptions are shared, can they be examined and tested.

As you may recall, Charlie, a member of Joe Smith's group, had a long-standing problematic relationship with his father. One day, some time after the dramatized "chair" incident, Charlie turned on Joe in fury and demanded that he stop shouting. "Don't yell at me or at anyone else because I won't stand for it anymore!" The group was struck dumb, whereupon Joe asked the members if anyone else had heard him shout. A protracted silence ensued. He persisted in inquiring of members how he had been talking. They agreed among themselves that it was in his normal tone of voice. Charlie now accused the entire group of being sycophants and in cahoots with the leader. Luckily for Charlie and his eventual learnings, the session was being tape-recorded and the scene could be replayed. Charlie remained silent and deep in thought for a long spell. His conflict with his father was by no means resolved there, but at least a step in that direction had been taken.

Joe, of course, did at times share his own perceptions with the group. In this particular instance, however, he had sensed that such sharing would simply antagonize Charlie without furthering his learnings. Gloria Brown's situation was different. After the role-play when Gloria had been accused of cruelty, her first impulse was to agree with the charge. But having listened to Gladys and the others, she felt she must, indeed wanted to, share her own perceptions with the group:

> Now that everyone who wished to has spoken, I'd like
> to present my side of the story. As far as that's con-
> cerned, I certainly didn't intend to be cruel, and, had
> I known what was coming, might even have decided
> against the play. But when you, Gladys, said what you
> did afterwards, I was glad I had suggested it. Anyway,
> I'm glad you were all straight with me.

Bob Jones tried very hard to share his perceptions with the committee. He always made it clear that these perceptions were his and that he did not wish to impose them on anyone, but that he shared them in the hope that others would be encouraged to do the same. There were not many repercussions to this, but not because Bob hadn't tried.

Frequently, the leader can elicit much useful information by encouraging members to share their perceptions of how the group has been learning. The leader may be way off the mark, assuming that members are progressing, whereas they feel they are bogged down. The opposite may also occur. Bill Thomas could not get a clear picture about the learnings of his group, and, one day, decided to ask them for their perceptions. At first, members had been reluctant to participate. They had not initiated membership in the group but had been coerced, albeit gently, into the group, which forced them to think seriously about their individual futures, rather than just kid around and hope for the best. If that was learning, then they were learning. However, most members expressed the view that this kind of group wasn't really the ultimate solution. Here at the Center, they knew each other's problems. They knew they were blind persons about to re-enter the world of the seeing. But that world was represented in the group only by Bill, and he, with all of his understanding and acceptance, was remaining right here at the Center. Members, therefore, proposed a different type of group — one in which the sighted would also participate: family, friends, potential employers. If they were supposed to integrate in the outside world, that integration should begin right here. Bill was impressed by their approach, and asked why they had not spoken up earlier, why they had not themselves initiated the matter. No one had a satisfactory explanation at first, but they began to realize that they had thought vaguely about it and only when Bill had asked for their perceptions regarding the group's work, had the idea fully crystallized.

I have already discussed the criteria for helpful feedback in Chapter 5. Here I wish to stress that most of us are not born with the ability to give and receive feedback. It is a skill that generally must be acquired. It can be practiced in the group if members become convinced of its importance, and if the leader is skillful in teaching it (Golembiewski and Blumberg, 1970, pp. 69–73). Feedback is a form of communication that provides me with information about how others perceive me. It can tell me what impact my behavior makes on participants in the group. Objectively speaking, all individuals interested in learning about their behavior and its effects on others should welcome such a rare opportunity. Where else but in the group do people take the trouble to be so forthright with each other? Who, outside the group, would be willing to stick their necks out to tell us frankly and specifically how they perceive us and how our behavior affects them? From whom would we be prepared to hear it — and under what circumstances? What motives might we attribute to them? And to whom outside of the group would we be prepared to give such feedback? Is it not simpler and less threatening all around to keep our respective impressions of each other to ourselves?

Therefore, when the opportunity does present itself, we hesitate, equivocate, display ambivalence. The group leader must anticipate our reservations and cope with them. Precisely because we seldom, if ever, receive and give helpful feedback elsewhere, the concept must be introduced gradually, and its purpose explained repeatedly. There is an additional reason for this gradualness: unless and until a climate of basic trust is established, there can and will be no honest feedback.

Bob Jones does a lot of work with teachers and student teachers. In his training he stresses the giving and receiving of feedback that is relevant to their perceptions of themselves and others as teachers or future teachers. One year he was the consultant for a newly established high school, whose staff wanted its new school to be as open as possible. Many of the teachers had transferred from traditionally oriented schools, and they felt they needed an in-service training program to help them focus on their teaching methods and style. Bob's group consisted of ten teachers who had volunteered for the program. They met one full day each week during the entire school year.

The program was designed to encompass two stages. During the first of these, teachers became better acquainted, decided on group goals, and began to learn to use feedback. Although cognizant that the distinction is not always clear, Bob suggested that members try to concentrate on those behaviors relevant to themselves as teachers. Once feedback criteria had been explained, clarified, and agreed on, Bob introduced feedback gradually into the group's work. The teachers did not find it an easy matter to describe rather than to evaluate behavior, their own included. Learning to be specific and clear proved less difficult for them. Appropriate timing was something of a problem initially because members tended to hesitate, and by the time feedback was tendered other interactions had intervened.

There was no overt opposition to feedback, and all members declared that it was for this very purpose they had come. Still, Bob suggested checking it out first with the member concerned, just in case. During these initial meetings, the group learned to work together. A friendly climate prevailed and basic trust was established. The envious attention the group received from nonparticipating faculty members helped it to coalesce rapidly; however, at a later point this very attention created some difficulties for the staff of the school.

During the second phase of the program, when members had become skillful in giving and receiving feedback, they visited classrooms to observe each other actually behaving as teachers. This was done only when a member had expressed his or her readiness to be observed. The purpose of these visits was explained to pupils before the observers arrived. Of course, only teachers participating in the program were observed. After each visit members of the group would meet to exchange their impressions, the observed teacher generally leading off. It is not surprising that this group did not wish to disband at the end of the school year.

HOW, NOT WHY

Joe Smith has a theory. He believes that patients, both on the ward and in the clinic, develop what he calls the "diagnosis syndrome." By this, he means that they pick up psychiatric jargon from the staff and from the psychiatric subject matter of the films they see. In his group he ceaselessly fought this affliction, insisting that diagnosis be left to the specialists, who themselves are not always of one mind. Group members should concentrate on the *how* of behavior, and leave the *why* alone. After Charlie's outburst, Charlie himself was quick to explain that it was because of his paranoid tendencies. Joe, ignoring this, asked Charlie how Charlie had perceived him when Charlie had accused him of shouting. How had he felt at the time, and how had he reacted to his own outburst?

One evening, a new member was added to this open group. No one welcomed Dave, and his occasional comments were not picked up. This behavior surprised Joe as hitherto the group had always focused its attention on new members, but for the time being he withheld comment. The group became entangled in a political discussion. Again, Dave's attempts to join in were disregarded. Joe now decided to share his own perceptions with the group; he pointed out their hostile attitude toward Dave, cited specific behaviors of rejection, and suggested that the political discussion had been purely evasion tactics. When the ensuing free-for-all had subsided to the point where individual members could be heard, it turned out that a member had overheard a staff doctor speak of Dave as a psychopath and had passed this information on to the group, which now wanted nothing to do with him. How Dave had, in fact, behaved in the group could not be described by a single group member. One had perceived him as monopolizing the discussion. Another said he looked dangerous. Nearly everyone agreed that Joe was to blame for the unpleasant incident, since he had brought a psychopath into the group.

During the second phase of Bob Jones's teacher group, when members sat in on each other's classes, Hilda's history class was among the first to be observed. Immediately after the lesson, the group gathered for a feedback session. Hilda told them that she had been glad to give in to the pupils' pressure to dismiss class fifteen minutes early so they could get to the basketball game on time. Had she refused, they would not have concentrated in any case, and some of the kids might have walked out. Anyway, the school she had attended hadn't even had a basketball team, and she was glad that this one did. After this exposition, those who had observed her class burst into laughter. Hilda blushed, and Bob, who had been unable this time to sit in on the observation, was totally mystified. When the laughter died down, the explanations came, and, for once, perceptions were almost identical. Hilda had told them she was glad, but she had neither sounded nor looked it. As a matter of fact, she had seemed rather annoyed during the shortened lesson. She had spoken rapidly, as if to make up for lost time, and had been impatient with questions and comments. On top of it all, at the end of the class she had made a "Freudian slip": "We'll start, I mean we'll stop now. I hope you enjoy the game."

LEADER BEHAVIORS AND ATTITUDES

If we are going to attempt to practice what we preach, we cannot afford to ignore theories, cognitive learnings, and research findings related to group work. But even less can we afford to ignore the way we ourselves behave in groups as well as the attitudes we hold about them, for it is these that will be analyzed by group members and checked against our verbal theorizing. It is just because we teach behaviors and attitudes that our own are so vulnerable to surveillance in the group, thus imparting to group work a special challenge for some leaders and a covert threat for others. I wish, therefore, to touch upon some leader behaviors and attitudes since, in the main, they are skills that can be acquired. Naturally, I fully realize the limitations of a written treatment of the subject, which can at best serve as an adjunct to experience.

Are leaders responsible for their groups? This is a complex philosophical issue that I shall deliberately avoid. Instead, let me state a few guidelines that are helpful to me. I completely disagree with the position that maintains that the leader is no more responsible for the group than any of its members. Having acted to set it up, or at least having agreed to lead it, a leader is, in my view, responsible for displaying the professional conduct of his or her particular training toward the group. Members have every right to expect the leader to halt any behavior that is potentially harmful to the group's welfare, damaging to its learnings, and deviant from those ethical standards that the leader's profession enjoins. Quite apart from these restrictions, much will happen in the group that the leader may disagree with or dislike. He or she is responsible for stating this if there is a possibility that silence from the leader would be equated with consent.

In the group, individual members are responsible for their behavior and for their learnings. Whether they speak up or remain silent, share their views and feelings or conceal them; whether they attend meetings or stay away, they are responsible for their own acts. They are also responsible for how they learn and how they interpret these learnings. As for the group, collectively it is responsible for the motivation and interest it brings to its work and also for the decisions it takes. An agency that sponsors a group and makes it possible for a leader to function directly or indirectly takes responsibility for this leader's professional qualifications and ethical standards. Society's responsibility lies in setting up and enforcing suitable standards of professional competence and behavior.

The leader is not responsible for how group goals are carried out, but is responsible for maintaining the basic framework in which these goals may be achieved. For example, there are people who join a limited goals group, such as a discussion group, who immediately attempt to burden all present with lengthy self-disclosures. When told that they are out of line, that the group's goals lie in another direction, it is not uncommon today for such members to counter that they are merely demonstrating trust, being open, and being authentic. This is an extreme case, but it shows that certain terms that have entered our daily vocabulary are often loosely defined and improperly used. In some groups, trust, openness, and authenticity constitute a goal in themselves; in others they are desirable but not essential; and, in others still, they are no more important than other highly valued human traits such as clarity, integrity, and competence. My purpose here is not to quibble over words, but to caution leaders that it is their responsibility to ensure these terms' proper use in the framework of the group.

I should like to emphasize that talking about trust will not produce it, that openness is not easily attained, and that authenticity is achieved by few people and not necessarily because they have participated in groups (Bugental, 1965). In a nutshell: if you mean it, be it, in and out of the group. This is especially true of leader behavior, for the worst enemies of group learnings are leader phoniness and incongruity.

Genuine trust takes a long time and much hard work to develop in the group. Members must get to know each other, be prepared to share with each other, acquire at least the basics of giving and receiving help and of feedback before they can really trust one another: trust based on honest self-disclosure and genuine self-exploration. Members cannot trust each other unless they basically accept and respect one another, and unless they are quite certain that they will be listened to and a sincere attempt be made to understand them. Trust grows with working and learning together in the group. There are no shortcuts; that is why trust, when achieved, is such a precious element of interpersonal relations.

Not all successful groups achieve trust. Trust did not develop in Bob's committee — in contrast to his teachers' group, where a great deal of trust did develop. Joe's group could not hope to develop trust fully as the membership, by definition of an open group, fluctuated. Bill's group was disbanded before the issue of trust arose, and as for Gloria, she was not sure to the very end whether members really trusted one another. It was discussed in the group now and again, and members rated their mutual trust on a scale ranging from "none" to "very high." Most checked "some."

Gimmicks not only cannot expedite trust, but they can make the entire trust issue look ridiculous and cheap, and can create immeasurable repercussions on the rest of group life. There is a tendency today to introduce exercises borrowed from sensitivity training, Gestalt theory, or transactional analysis into more mundane group life. One exercise in particular is presumed to promote trust among members. They form a circle, standing close to one another.

The members, one after the other, are supposed to step to the center of the ring and let themselves fall backwards. The point of the exercise seems to be that if members can allow themselves to fall backwards, this signifies that they trust the group not to let them hit the floor. Well, I have yet to see even a group of complete strangers willingly let others break their necks.

Various currents can be distinguished within the movement of group life, and these occur in leaders as well. They may sense themselves drawn toward a group, away from it, or even against it. Behaviors in certain groups may lead leaders to recoil; other behaviors will propel them forward; others, again, may cause them to feel cold or antagonistic. If leaders experience feelings such as these, and the feelings persist long enough for leaders to become fully aware of them, they may decide to communicate the feelings to their groups as *their* feelings, as information their groups may want to examine, to sidestep, or to ignore entirely.

After struggling with his feelings for some time, Bob confessed to the members of the committee:

> I've often urged you to express your feelings about this group. Now I want to share some of mine. Some mornings before our sessions, I find myself waiting for a phone call canceling the meeting. I feel myself more and more distant from the group, and sometimes at night, just before going off to sleep, I find myself saying harsh things to you. I like and respect each of you individually, but, as a group, I feel you are keeping me at arm's length and I am beginning to resent it. I'm telling you this because I want you to know just how I feel, and because it may help you to analyze what is going on in the group.

When his teachers' group neared termination, and members were summing up their experiences and learnings, Bob joined in with:

> I've gotten to feel very close and warm toward this group, and I know I'm going to miss our weekly sessions. You have really learned to communicate with one another and I hope you can keep it up. We'll probably be seeing each other around next term, since I'll again be consulting at the school.

Right after the uproar following the Gladys–Fred role-play, Gloria experienced a distinct sensation, which she decided to share with the group:

> Right now I get the feeling that you are all drawing very close. It somehow reminds me of kids who are sorry about what they've done, and now want to make up with Mother.

Similar waves of movement toward, away from, and against the group and leader occur, of course, in individual members. They should be encouraged to express these feelings, which represent information the group requires. In Bill's group, Betty once told Archie that she felt he was a million miles away, uninterested in what the group was talking about but not willing to tell what was bothering him. Archie agreed with her, but said it was just a mood and he didn't want to talk about it in the group, so that ended the matter. Some time after the cold reception given Dave when he joined Joe's group, when terminology had been clarified and tempers cooled, Dave admitted that when he first entered the group, he felt quite friendly toward everyone, but after their reaction he had been ready to choke practically each and every member. Now he felt sort of stuck, not ready to get too close, for fear of being hurt again, and yet not willing to leave the group.

The last behavior I wish to mention here is one with which neophyte group leaders are already familiar from their previous professional training and background: helping a person to change. Whatever "school" they are affiliated with, they probably try to help people change in the dyadic relationship through some form of self-examination followed by understanding, and leading, eventually, to action and altered behavior based on these learnings (Carkhuff, 1971). These same methods are applicable in group work but with one significant difference: in the dyad this is what we do nearly all the time; in the group we are more selective.

Here again, leader style and group goals determine much of the outcome. If leaders work almost exclusively with their groups as a whole, they will initiate little in the way of a dyadic relationship with any one member. If the focus is on the individual — as it tends to be in group psychotherapy — leaders may work with member after member, always leaving room for group interactions and group participation. They will probably not concentrate on any one member too long at a stretch, but return to specific members when issues pertaining to them arise in the group.

The transfer of the dyadic relationship into the group is intended to be helpful to all members even though, for the moment, the focus is on only one. By working with Gladys, Gloria wants especially to help her. In addition, she hopes that the interchange will trigger off a reaction in other group members, so that they too will wish to join in helping Gladys to examine her behavior and understand how it affects others. What is even more important to Gloria is that the dyadic exchange may encourage other members to greater self-disclosure in the group so that, gradually, every group member will be involved almost simultaneously in giving help to others and receiving it from them. In this sense, what Gloria is practicing with Gladys is a form of behavior modeling. If she succeeds, group members will be at the same time pupils and teachers, learning and teaching together with her.

COMMUNICATION

Everything that happens in groups, in one way or another, constitutes communication. Three of the most important skills of leaders are the ability to **manage** this communication, to **interpret** it, and, when necessary, to **guide** it into more effective channels. Whether managing, interpreting, or guiding, leaders act in terms of their own perceptions, and they may wish to share these in order to explain their actions and to invite reactions.

The leader **manages** communication in the group by open or subtle behaviors. A leader employs clear management signals such as, "Well, I suppose we might just as well begin even though Alice hasn't arrived yet"; or "We'll have to stop now. We can pick up from here next time, if you like."

Or, in a slightly different context, the leader might say:

> Anyone want to add anything? Well, I guess no one does. Perhaps you want to think over what we've been saying to you, Joan — we can get back to it another time. [silence] Anybody have any suggestions as to what to talk about next time?

More subtle management on the leader's part might be:
>By the look on your face, Charlie, I see you have more
>to say. Now, I don't know if you are ready to say it;
>I do know that I'm ready to listen, and I'm sure the
>group is, too.

It often occurs that members consistently direct their remarks to the leader. In such cases, a leader's cue to them might be to remain silent, in the hope that someone else in the group will react, thus avoiding a situation in which communication is always channeled through the leader. On the other hand, a leader may prefer, especially in early meetings of the group, to come out with it openly:

>I've noticed, and perhaps some of the group have too,
>that some people always address their comments to
>me. Since I want to encourage you to interact, I won't
>always respond. I'll have my say, too, when it is rele-
>vant, but I'd rather we didn't set up a pattern in this
>group whereby all communication goes through me.

At times, management of communication involves teaching:
>I can detect three conversations going on simultane-
>ously. We can't possibly hear what everyone is trying
>to say. How do you think we can solve this communi-
>cation problem?

In the course of **interpreting** communication, the leader focuses on both the verbal and nonverbal cues given by members. The leader may interpret, elicit interpretations from the group, or work toward a joint effort of group and leader. Joe Smith is especially sensitive to **nonverbal cues,** those hints we communicate to others by tone of voice, posture, body movements, and facial expression (Middleman, 1970).

He said once:
>I've been noticing, Dave, that whenever you talk you
>bow your head and look at the floor. This gives me a
>feeling that it's as if you were telling us that you're
>kind of ashamed of what you're saying, and that you
>are asking us to excuse you for saying it.

At another point Joe said:

> When you said that you don't care how they treat you,
> Mary, your voice sounded much angrier to me than
> your words. To tell the truth, I don't know which to
> believe — the words or the tone.

Interpretations of verbal behaviors may revolve around group participation and interaction. They may focus on who talks, how often, how long, to whom, after whom, and so on. Bill Thomas once faced his rehabilitants with:

> I don't know whether you have paid any attention to
> this, but I get a pretty clear picture that there are
> certain people in the group who always speak up just
> after someone in particular has said something. It's
> as if some people triggered others off. Did you no-
> tice who just talked after whom? Has this happened
> before?

Some groups learn to interpret verbal and nonverbal cues alone and no longer need the leader to get the ball rolling. In Gloria Brown's group, Sylvia once addressed Ruth:

> When you were talking to Jack you kept glancing over
> at Louise, and she kind of smiled back at you. I had
> the impression you were telling her how brave you
> thought you were, saying all that to Jack, and her
> smile meant "Keep it up, let him have it; I'm with
> you." It's as if both of you were ganging up on him
> though just one was doing the talking.

Bob Jones's group of teachers became very interested in interpret-ing communication as they learned to appreciate its relevance to their work in the classroom. During one of their weekly meetings, the following interchange occurred:

> *Dana*
> We're getting to be more independent as a group. We
> don't all look at Bob so often anymore for approval.
>
> *Jerry*
> I agree with you, but look at the way you're holding
> your hands . . . [laughter] . . . yeah, just like Bob.

Bob

I suppose we all imitate one another. When we go to observe Dana in her biology class today, perhaps we will see some kids imitating some of *her* behaviors. Anyone interested in looking out for that?

During the course of group meetings, the leader will at times find it necessary to **guide** the group's transition from one level of communication to another. Bob, for example, tried repeatedly to move his committee from **content** to **process** considerations:

Although the content of our discussion regarding the impact of salary differentials on motivation is very absorbing, I've also been interested in watching *how* the group has gone about this task. I wonder whether anyone else has been focusing on the process angle. Did anyone notice, for example, who looked at whom, who tended to talk, and who took no part at all in the discussion? I thought I saw Pete watching Ted for the last few minutes. Stan, you kept pretty much out of things. Instead of just my rambling on, perhaps some of you have noticed things dealing with process?

Task and **maintenance** issues in the group had caused Bill much concern at the beginning. The group had just not known how to spend its time profitably. The life plan idea had solved the task issue. Now Bill felt free to focus on maintenance considerations. During a particularly tense meeting, he commented:

I suppose we all felt the tension in the group while Joan was telling about her plan. I think you're now bombarding her with questions which she can't possibly answer all at once. There's lots of fidgeting going on and people seem restless. Clark has even left his seat and is wandering about the room. Perhaps, if we can just get some of these feelings out into the open, we can help Joan know what's bothering us.

J. R. Gibb discusses communication in terms of two very distinct and even contrasting climates that prevail in groups (Gibb, 1961). He speaks of a "defensive" as opposed to a "supportive" climate that can, to a greater or lesser degree, be discerned in groups. In the former, members tend to evaluate communication rather than describe it. The defensive climate stresses control, whereas the supportive climate is problem oriented. In the former, people seem to be concerned primarily with strategy, while in the latter they allow themselves to be more spontaneous. When people are defensive in their communication, they remain uninvolved and impersonal. When they are supportive, they empathically try to see things as the speaker sees them, and are prepared to state how they themselves see, feel, and react to what is occurring. In the defensive climate, the superiority of some members over others and the leader over them all is made evident; in the supportive climate an atmosphere of equality is encouraged. And, finally, certitude and explicitness tend to predominate in the former whereas in the latter, participants can tolerate a measure of ambiguity and accept provisional findings and conclusions.

THE RIGHT TO DISBAND

In concluding this chapter, I should like to discuss a skill leaders will have to learn to apply occasionally, even though and partly because it is hurtful to their pride and self-esteem. This skill involves the recognition of the group's right to disband. Most group leaders, like most other people, do not enjoy being rejected. But group leaders must subordinate their personal needs to those of the group, and, in any case, should recognize that when a group decides to disband, it is not necessarily rejecting its leader.

When a group is set up, there is no guarantee that it will function successfully. Its composition may be unfortunate, its motivation low, its goals unclear. When a leader is chosen to work with a group — whether it be by the leader's institution or by the members themselves — no assurance exists that they will hit it off together. The leader must become sensitive to the functioning of the group and to his or her role in it, so that both factors can be appraised, as well as their mutual interaction. The leader should act for the good of the group, without becoming either its martyr or its exploiter.

Group members are generally hesitant about facing up to their discontent with the leader or their desire to break up. They are often reluctant to reveal their feelings on these matters to the leader or to other group members, for fear of hurting them. They do not realize that by remaining silent, they may in the long run hurt them much more and, in the bargain, go on suffering unnecessarily themselves. It is, therefore, up to the leader to test skillfully and tactfully the members' wishes to remain together as a group and their degree of satisfaction with their leader. This, of course, is easier said than done, since it often requires a good deal of time before a group can really tell that they cannot possibly work together or with their leader. The situation becomes more complicated still when everyone realizes that the group has no alternative; for example, it may be a team whose composition is a given factor, or else no other leader may be available. Even then, it may be preferable to disband the group. The matter is far from simple.

In groups in which membership is decided on a nonvoluntary basis, it may be mandatory to make the best of the matter. In this case, the leader will have to be prepared to work on the problem with the group before other matters can be tackled. Bill's rehabilitants expressed no desire to become a group and were somewhat resentful when the matter was decided for them. Bill was able to help them discover a task that held their interest and enabled them to function as a group. Bob found himself in a much more difficult position with his committee. On many occasions he attempted to raise the matter of the members' ambivalence toward working together. As we have seen, they consistently sidestepped the issue until the group broke up without having openly discussed its difficulties even once.

When a group is set up whose members are strangers to each other, they need time to become acquainted. Most groups of this kind learn to live with fellow members and the leader. Occasionally, a member will drop out for one reason or another, but very rarely does such an impasse occur between the group and the leader that they cannot go on together. I am assuming, of course, that the leader is professionally trained and, if a neophyte in group work, is receiving the necessary supervision and support.

I was once asked to consult with a kibbutz work team. Although we all tried very hard, it soon became evident that because of existing frictions on the kibbutz itself, the group could not fruitfully work together. We consequently decided to disband. Early in our relationship, I had become aware of the team's inability to function properly but had concluded, erroneously as it turned out, that the problem lay with me. On another occasion, I was invited to work with a group of new immigrants from English-speaking countries. After two or three meetings this particular group showed its dissatisfaction, and did not hide the fact that group members thought I was not the right person to help them. Eventually, they found a leader more suited to their needs and were able to continue their work. Needless to say, I learned a good deal from this experience about myself as a person and as a leader.

7

The Group in Action

GROUP DEVELOPMENT

As groups develop, so much occurs that it is difficult and even, at times, impossible for leaders to keep track of everything at once. Fortunately, when members become more familiar with one another and learn to work toward a common goal, leaders can allow themselves to direct less and to participate more freely since members are now less dependent on them. Yet, they must try at all times to remain aware of the many nuances that occur in their groups. Because the picture before leaders is so often confused and overwhelming, it will be useful for them to keep in mind certain key questions pertaining to group development.

1. *Is the group moving toward its long range goals?* Are these clear and acceptable to all members? How are the group's immediate goals being dealt with? Would it be helpful to refocus on goals now and then? How about group versus individual goals — do they conflict or are they complementary? Is goal achievement still the goal?

2. *How much, if any, additional structuring is needed?* Are structure and setting congenial to the group? Are there attempts to rebel against them, and if so, is this indirectly resistance to the leader? Should structure be changed in order to accommodate certain members? If so, what about the rest? What might this mean for the group's setting? What do tardiness, absences, early departures indicate? Should the leader bring these to the group's attention or wait until members bring up the subject? If the group is part of an institutional framework, does the members' relation to the group setting show anything about their relation to the entire institution? Should this be brought into the open?

3. *What norms has the group established?* Were norms reached by consensus or by the control of a few over the many? Are they

being lived up to by everyone? How are deviates dealt with in the group? Are members fully conscious of group norms? Are these norms hampering or facilitating group development? What is the leader's role as regards group norms, and how do they affect him or her?

4. *What kind of communication network has the group set up?* How does information flow? Does it reach all members? Who tends to communicate with whom? To avoid whom? Have subgroups sprung up, and, if so, have they developed their own internal communication network? What is the leader's place in the communication network? Are there, in the group, gatekeepers to communication? Gate-sealers? Does the communication pattern tend to favor some members over others? Has it altered during the group's development? Does it need improving, streamlining?

5. *Are member roles fixed, or do group members feel free to adopt roles appropriate to specific situations?* Are there members who are particularly concerned about the group's maintenance needs in addition to its goal achievement? How are maintenance needs understood and satisfied? Are the maintenance people looked upon as softies, time wasters, obstructors? How do they conduct themselves in the group? Is the group concentrating on its task and ignoring personal needs and feelings? Should the leader intervene now or wait?

6. *How is the group dealing with conflict?* Is antagonism being openly expressed? Is there conflict over task or maintenance issues, or both? How are conflicts dealt with? Are they faced, ignored, sidestepped, whitewashed, treated as part of problem solving? Does there exist conflict between members and leader? Are personal antagonisms interfering with task achievement? Is the leader expected to solve conflicts? What is the leader's attitude toward conflict?

7. *What about authority issues in the group?* Is the leader still the one and only authority, or have other authority figures arisen in the group? Are members competing for authority among themselves? Are they competing with the leader? Are members submissive, rebellious, independent? Do members recognize different loci of authority?

8. *How are decisions reached in the group?* If decisions are imposed, who imposes them? Are decisions reached with, against, or apart from the leader? Are they reached spontaneously or after long deliberation? Are they carried out, forgotten, distorted in execution? Does the group resort to voting or does it try to reach a consensus? How does it go about this?

9. *What about group morale?* Are members glad to get together? Do they seem happy to leave? Are people task oriented, or do they primarily care about each other as persons? Does the group prefer play or work? Does group morale rise and fall rapidly or does it stay pretty even? What affects group morale? Are there certain members who influence it more than others?

10. *Is the group on the lookout for new perceptions?* Is feedback being used, and if so, is it helpful? Are new perceptions invited, tolerated, or resented? Who offers new perceptions to the group readily? Who with hesitancy? Who not at all?

11. *Has the group entrapped its members?* Has the group's existence become an end in itself? Are members building a mystique about their group? Are they becoming addicted to the group? Are they attributing to it an identity of its own, way beyond the members composing it? What is the leader's role in this development? Is the leader using the group to fulfill his or her personal needs?

12. *Are people learning in the group?* Is the level of tension conducive to learning? Who generates the tension? Are members paying lip service to learnings, or are they prepared to examine these openly in the group? Are they learning what the leader hoped they would learn? Who contributes new ideas, new understandings? Who is beginning to behave differently, to enlarge his or her frame of reference, to express new attitudes? Does all of this learning sound genuine or phony to the leader, to members?

13. *How do members see the leader's behavior?* Does the leader appear consistent? Evoke trust? Genuinely care for the group and its members? Is the leader perceived as an authentic person? Is the leader congruent?

Questions such as these should concern us — before, during, and after group meetings — but not at the expense of our immediacy and spontaneity. It is somewhat like drawing up a balance sheet of group life or a profile of group development, if only a provisional one.

GROUP HISTORY

At this point I will stress the obvious, simply because it is so often forgotten, overlooked, or neglected in group work: every group, certainly every closed group, develops its own history. I am certain that it is rewarding for leader and member alike to become aware of this history-building process and to engage in examining it. The group's history is documented through diaries, notes, tapes, recollections, and even fantasies. The group should not, of course, become compulsively concerned with its history or narcissistic about its own development, for in that case it will produce very little new history. But it should refer to its history now and again in order to realize that the group is growing, and to realize that it has a past that influences the present, both of which are bound to affect its future. The study of history is a cohesive element in the life of an individual; it is no less so in the life of a group. Let me present an example taken from Bob's teachers' group.

During a session in the middle period of the group's life, when members were discussing the teaching of history, Barbara, a history teacher, suggested that since the group itself was in the process of developing a history, it might want to take the opportunity to delve into it. Members brought diaries, notes, and the few tapes they had recorded to the next meeting. Barbara proposed that everyone relate incidents from the group's past and illustrate these, whenever possible, with excerpts from the documents. Important group events stood out clearly. While these were occurring, members had perceived them from their own frame of reference. Now, in retrospect, these events were reassessed to the degree that it seemed, at times, that they had taken place in a different group or even in different groups. Hank's "forgetting" to come to the first meeting was remembered by all. Back then people had been quite angry with him. Now everyone knew that it was typical of Hank: what he did not write down he forgot, and whatever he did not look at, once written down, ceased to exist. Some could not fathom, others resented, and still others admired Hank's lackadaisical attitude. But all knew him better now and were familiar with other of his behaviors, including the trouble he had taken to locate a suitable meeting place for the group in the crowded school building.

The note of nostalgia dissipated quickly when members recalled Bob's outburst at their third meeting. He had accused them of being closed and uptight, and only, as it later transpired, because he had felt aggressive toward another group. The outburst had truly shocked them, but Bob's honesty, when confronted by astonished members, had impressed them. From then on, the word *projection* had come to hold a very special meaning for the group.

Members recalled how, during early meetings, they had drawn closer together through sharing their previous experience as teachers before they had joined the staff of this school, and through describing their diverse educational backgrounds and training. This had been one of Bob's early suggestions. Interest had evoked further discussion, and soon they were speaking about future plans, hopes, and expectations.

An event that had appeared insignificant at the time had taken on new proportions since; they had all read the same book for a particular meeting, but when they began to discuss it, one might have thought they were discussing several, very different books. Marian now related that, just the other day, her pupils had understood one of her assignments in such diverse ways that, from their homework, she had found it almost impossible to recognize what she had assigned. Although members thought that Marian was exaggerating somewhat, they could empathize with her while enjoying the story.

Renée recalled the first time group members had come to her class to observe. It hadn't felt at all like a supervisor's visit since group members were friends and peers, but, nevertheless, they were competitors as well. She recalled how they had held back at first from criticizing, from making even the most noncommittal remarks. Today they knew more about classroom observation, about feedback, and, of course, felt much freer with one another, but the visits were still a strain. Perhaps with time and more experience the visits would become easier.

Some groups that are on the verge of terminating get bogged down in relating incidents from the past. It gives the group something to hang onto at a time when it is hard to know what to speak of, but at this late stage it seldom furthers learnings and generally is only the start of a nostalgic romanticizing about the group and its past.

My point is that the group's history can be employed quite otherwise: to review the past at an earlier stage, when it may help us
understand our present better in order that we may plan jointly the
future we desire for our group.

IS THE LEADER A MEMBER?

Frequently during early meetings, leaders' positive attributes tend
to be exaggerated in the eyes of their groups. They are seen as all-
powerful, omniscient, and, at times, all-loving. When this over-
enthusiastic phase wanes, it may well be replaced by one of let-
down: the leaders have faults, they err, they are far from knowing
everything, and, even worse, are by no means all-loving. Eventually,
this awakening to reality, rather painful at first, gives way to seeing
leaders more or less as they really are — more or less ordinary people with shortcomings and hang-ups of their own. By now, their
groups are ready to accept them as one of the crowd, as just another member.

The question "Is the leader a member of the group?" deserves
careful consideration. My answer is an unqualified no. Leaders are
by no means members of the groups they lead. In undertaking to
function as leaders of groups, they have accepted a task in their
professional capacity, a task for which they are generally paid a
fee.* The need of groups to inflate the image of the leader, sub-
sequently to deflate it, and eventually to perceive the leader as being
one of them does not justify leaders wavering in their role. Just the
opposite is true. When leaders and members draw closer to each
other, new problems arise. Can they really be tackled if the leader
disappears and re-emerges as just another member? As distance is
reduced and intimacy increases, barriers tend to fall. Which barriers
should they be?

Roles arouse expectations and impose responsibilities. The parent
who wishes to be a buddy to her child instead of being "merely"

---

* I do not discuss fees in this book as my own preference is to receive re-
muneration directly from the institutions that set up groups. Thus, I have had
very little personal experience in the matter of fees, and since this text is
based largely on my own personal learnings, I refer the reader to the literature dealing with the subject (Yalom, 1975).

a parent will soon find herself in a quandary. The teacher who needs to be a pal to his pupils will mislead them, and eventually hurt and disappoint both them and himself. The employees whose boss wants them to like her for what she is and to forget she is their employer may find themselves out of a job before they have realized that pleasant as she may be, the boss remains the boss. So, let parents and children enjoy a close relationship, let teachers enable pupils to approach them and to feel free and open with them, let employers be humane and fair in their dealings with employees — but let them all take care not to forget that they are fulfilling specific roles, lest illusions be created that may cause everyone to suffer in the long run.

In speaking of the role of the leader, I do not mean to refer to any specific leadership style. How leaders fulfill their role — in an authoritarian, distant, group-centered, friendly, neutral, or any other style — is important but not directly related to the issue at hand. All leaders bring into groups with them certain idiosyncrasies and hang-ups. These should not be allowed to hinder them in fulfilling the leader role to which they are bound until group life terminates.

When, during an early meeting with his teachers' group, Bob burst out in anger, he was introducing his own problems into the group. He was transferring his perceptions and frustrations regarding the committee to another group, where they did not belong. The teachers were aghast. Later, when Bob realized what had happened to him, he was able to explain to the group, and no permanent damage was done. However, it would have been far better had he been able to rid himself of his bitter emotions in the appropriate place.

Once leaders fully grasp their role and their responsibilities, it is a great deal easier for them to function adequately. They most assuredly play a part in the shaping of the histories and development of the groups they conduct, and to that extent they are participants in group events. They are, in a manner of speaking, of groups but not in them. They are part of the ongoing process and thus contribute to it, but always with the aim of promoting the learnings of their groups and helping them to attain their goals. Here again, we can compare the group leader to the conductor of the orchestra: everyone plays together and all have the same goal in view, but the performance is best if everyone keeps in mind the unique role of the conductor and behaves accordingly.

RESPONSES

As the group develops, member actions and interactions tend to increase in quantity and complexity. There are systems that categorize such actions and interactions to assist leader and members alike in organizing the seeming chaos of interactions, and to focus on those that are of major importance in a group's evolution at any given time. The system I recommend for the neophyte group leader is that of Bales (Bales et al., 1965; Bales, 1970; Golembiewski and Blumberg, 1970, p. 154). This category system is comprised of twelve responses: six of which Bales calls "emotional," and the other six "problem solving." They are so basic and so clearly delineated that they require no further explanation. I state them in the order and form that I prefer.

A. Emotionally positive responses
    1. shows solidarity, helps
    2. shows tension release, laughs
    3. agrees

B. Emotionally negative responses
    4. shows antagonism
    5. shows tension
    6. disagrees

C. Problem-solving responses, questions
    7. asks for suggestion
    8. asks for opinion
    9. asks for orientation, information

D. Problem-solving responses, answers
    10. gives suggestion
    11. gives opinion
    12. gives orientation, information

As can be seen from the above, Bales limits himself to three emotional responses: displaying solidarity or antagonism, revealing or releasing tension, and agreeing or disagreeing. He limits his problem-solving responses to three, as well: giving or asking for suggestion, providing or requesting opinion, and furnishing or requesting information. In this concentrated form, the neophyte need pay attention to only six responses in the group. These seem simple enough, but, unless they are mastered, it will be impossible to go on to other significant responses that are not so easily categorized. Even the basic six dimensions can be enlarged on; members do not only give or request information. They may, for example, withhold it, remain indifferent, or reject it when it is offered. Members will not only show tension or release tension: there are other alternatives as well. However, once these six categories have become part of leaders' cognitive equipment, they will expand them as required by their groups' needs and their own inclinations.

I cannot resist adding a personal note. I always get very annoyed in the group when a suggestion is sought and, after some hesitation, one is offered in good faith by a member. Frequently, the next thing that happens will be that the other members insist that it is up to the member who made the suggestion to carry it out. To me this seems not only totally unwarranted but also logically unsound. The group asks for suggestions and a member complies. In what way does that even imply that that member must be the one to carry it out? On the contrary, it is now up to the group to weigh, accept, reject, or modify the suggestion. This accomplished, they must decide collectively how to continue from there. It is my belief that valuable suggestions are often withheld from the group because individual members do not feel ready to carry out alone the suggestions they would otherwise be happy to offer.

FEELINGS

In all the groups thus far alluded to in the text, as well as in those with which I have been privileged to work, feelings have evolved as a central issue of group life. Each of us possesses feelings and deals with them in one way or another. One of the reasons for participating in a group may be the desire to become more aware of one's feelings, to experience them more fully, and to learn to deal with them in new ways — ways that may prove more satisfying and life enhancing. There is, of course, much more to life than feelings, but life without them would be empty, indeed.

I can conceal my feelings or face them. I can deny them or project them on others. I can act them out or express them verbally. What I can learn in the group is, first of all, to allow myself to fully experience my feelings; second, to become completely aware of them, and third, to decide what to do about them. I may feel ashamed, guilty, proud, uneasy, or be ambivalent about my feelings. I may experience mixed feelings at times and, as a consequence, become confused. There are feelings I may try to ignore and others I may try to flee from. Some feelings I will want to keep to myself, but others I will want to share.

The patients in Joe's group learned gradually that feelings are not taboo, that everyone possesses them and can learn to accept them and to experience them more fully. They also learned that feeling is not synonymous with acting. It took Charlie some time till he could admit to himself the hatred he felt toward his father. For years he had been so afraid of the violence of his feelings that he attempted to stifle them and pretend they did not exist. In the group, he was amazed to discover that he was not alone in his hatred, and that others hated too: a parent, a sibling, even a renowned public figure. Charlie began to realize that he had transferred some of his hatred to Joe, but that Joe, far from reciprocating it, did not even wish to punish him for his hostile feelings. Group members did not despise him either. On the contrary, they drew closer to him and tried to help.

And then a very strange thing happened. As other members began to speak of their parents and of their childhood memories, Charlie suddenly recalled all sorts of incidents that he had not thought of in ages — incidents in which his father had played a role, but not the oppressive one he had remembered years later. Charlie experienced utter confusion. And then, when Joe and the group began speaking of ambivalent feelings, things became clearer. The story is familiar. Charlie still hated his father when he left the group, but it was not the same intense, all-absorbing hatred. Now he could admit to himself that he did, in fact, hate his father but that he experienced other, more positive feelings toward him as well. He no longer saw his father in other people. He still felt uneasy with the hatred but could now live better with it.

What Bill's blind rehabilitants liked most about him was his readiness to try to understand them without pressuring them. Bill had not worked with blind people before; as a matter of fact, he had never known a blind person. He was genuinely interested in the life plans the group presented, but it did not take long for him to realize that the members were not inclined to delve into their feelings. They had done too much of that already — among themselves, in individual counseling, in school, in the hospital. They had not asked for this group but were willing to cooperate as long as this did not involve going over ground that had been repeatedly covered. Altogether, the group was designed to last for only eight sessions, and the life plan idea suited everyone. Bill could respect the members' right not to express feelings in the group beyond what they themselves were ready for.

Bob's committee members never did express the feelings they experienced about each other and about him. Hence these could not be examined or dealt with in any way. Bob could only point out to them repeatedly what they were not doing, and reiterate why, in his opinion, this avoidance might hinder them in pursuing their declared goals. When the committee broke up, he was left with very mixed feelings of his own.

THE UNINVITED GUEST

Social norms and customs in most parts of the world would have us make the best of uninvited guests. We pretend to be glad to see them, feign interest in their well-being, find them a place at the table or near the hearth — in short, make them welcome. Not so in the closed group. After its initial trial run, the group settles down to an ordered existence with a stable and agreed-upon membership. Very true, you will contend, but in that case there can be no question of guests, whether they are invited or uninvited. And yet . . . well, let us see.

Concerning invited guests, I have known groups that have invited a guest to attend one or sometimes even more than one meeting for a very defined purpose. From our illustrative groups, two instances come to mind. Bill's group decided to invite the Center's director to meet with it, in order to discuss the role of the Center in the lives of rehabilitants after their return home. Bob's teachers asked to meet with the principal of the school so as to acquaint him with their activities and learnings, with a view to encouraging him to set up an additional group as soon as funds would permit.

But uninvited guests do appear in groups. It is a comparatively rare occurrence, but it happens. Let me cite two examples from my own experience and show how they were handled.

I recently worked with members of the psychiatric staff of a hospital. Participants in the group were chosen with great care in order to include or exclude staff members according to previously agreed-upon criteria. The group met once weekly. One day, to everyone's surprise, a young doctor walked in, introduced herself to the leader (everyone else knew her), and sat down. She informed me that she had just begun her internship in psychiatry at the hospital, had heard about the group's existence, and here she was. Utter silence ensued. The group was flabbergasted. I knew it was up to me to set things straight, to remove the pressure from the group without hurting the young doctor. Continued silence. Finally I spoke, explaining to her the goals of the group and the way it had been set up. I stressed that it was a closed group and that it had already developed a history. I had nothing against her personally, but nevertheless I must ask her to leave. I was really sorry. Someone in the group muttered that it was all a misunderstanding and that she should have been told beforehand. She got up and left.

Some time ago, I worked with a group of kibbutz members who had been elected to serve in central positions in their community for a period of two years. They wished to improve their interpersonal communication so as to serve their community more productively. After a couple of meetings the membership was determined, and the group began to work in weekly sessions. One day, as we arrived at our assigned meeting place, we found a newcomer seated there. Members whispered something to him; he did not budge. I introduced myself and inquired as to his purpose in coming. He replied, simply, that he was a member of the kibbutz, had heard about this group, and had decided to join. The group became ill at ease. I attempted to explain, to point out, to emphasize — all to no avail. He claimed that no closed group could possibly be set up on the kibbutz. Now members joined in the dialogue. All the explanations were once again gone over: he was not in an elected position that year, the group's goals were set up for a closed group. The uninvited guest stood firm. Some members began to weaken and suggested that, perhaps, after all . . . he was a respected and veteran member of the community . . . there was room. Others were infuriated, insisting that if he was admitted to the group, they would walk out. In short, the entire session was devoted to the uninvited guest, who left, obviously incensed, after an hour of futile bargaining.

In both instances I attempted to help the group maintain the composition it had agreed upon. It was obvious to all concerned that it would be easier for me, as least involved with the uninvited guests, to expel them — as gently as possible, but nevertheless to expel them.

In whatever manner expulsion of a nongroup member is done, the intruder will be upset; hence, the action should be swift. Ignoring the presence of a nonmember is far worse, since everyone feels uncomfortable, the group cannot possibly function adequately, guilt feelings develop on all sides, and, in the end, the uninvited guest has to leave anyway. The leader's role is not always a pleasant one.

PEOPLE ARE DIFFERENT

Let me close this chapter with a very obvious statement, one which, nevertheless, is not always easy to accept: people are different. I think we should rejoice in this, and stress the differences in our work, emphasizing how they can strengthen the group and help it to achieve its goals, especially when these differences are accepted and utilized for individual and group gain. We perceive differently; we think differently; we react differently. We do not share identical feelings and do not experience them at the same time; we all have distinct preferences and possess very individual strengths and weaknesses. We can learn in groups to appreciate just how very different we are, and yet how much we hold in common — including the desire to grow in directions truly meaningful to us as individuals. Only when we become fully aware of our differences, can we decide what we wish to share in common and what we are wiling to try in order to bring about change in ourselves.

By revealing our behavior to others in the group and learning about theirs, we are actually presented with alternatives of behavior from which to choose. We cannot become someone else, but we can, after learning more about others and ourselves, become more our own selves. Helpful feedback is offered in the group essentially to provide information regarding how others see me, perceive my behaviors, interpret my actions. What I do with this information is then entirely up to me. When Mary is told that she seems dependent and the reason she seems that way; when Jack learns that he is overprotecting his son because, deep down, he is jealous of him; when Betty realizes she is using her blindness to control people — only

Mary, Jack, and Betty can decide if and how to profit from these learnings. The frequently implied "I would like you better if . . ." or "You'd be better off were you to . . ." is present but the choice is up to the learner.

Every group consists of some members who are dominant and others who are more compliant. Even when made aware of this, the individuals involved do not always wish to change. Some people find it easier to express affection than hostility, whereas others lean in the opposite direction. Charlie was, at first, so full of hostility that he could not express any feelings whatsoever. Once the hostility had surfaced, he was able after a while to express affection as well.

Some group members have a tendency to lean unduly on others. Their dependence seems strange to those who like to make up their own minds at all times. Others still are basically dependent, and yet feel the need to hide this by refusing or rejecting any behavior that might possibly be construed by others as dependent. Gloria, in describing Ruth's counterdependent behavior, told her that she seemed very dependent on her husband and so resentful of the fact that she needed to oppose out-of-hand everything her husband wished or suggested.

Some members are oriented to achievement, others to affiliation, and still others to power. Some know this about themselves and accept it. Others become more fully aware of the one-sidedness of their behavior through the group and, as a result, seek more balance in their lives. Others, still, are so conflicted and frustrated that they will probably go on being so after the group disbands.

To illustrate, let me recount a short incident dealing with the power motif. I once asked members of a group to rank themselves in terms of their perceptions of member contributions to the group. They were to form a straight line with the member contributing most at the head and the one contributing least at the end of the line. There was to be no talking during the exercise, but members could move each other from position to position on the line until everyone was satisfied with his or her place and that of all the others. A discussion of the events was to follow. This group included two male members who were very active and power conscious. How would they act? Well, they jointly pushed into the number one position a rather neutral member, and placed themselves, very close together, in positions two and three! The exercise over, there was plenty to talk about.

Some group members do not reveal their true intentions immediately but employ what are known as "hidden agendas" (Schein and Bennis, 1967). Only if and when these are uncovered, does the group understand what those members really had in mind. When Andrew, who was generally quite active in the therapy group, had remained silent during two consecutive meetings, Joe asked him if he was prepared to explain his silence. Andrew replied that he felt he had talked so much in previous meetings that he wanted to see whether he could keep quiet for a change and listen to the others. Dick, who was sensitive to nonverbal cues, remarked that he didn't see it that way. To him, Andrew had seemed restless during the past two meetings and had been constantly scowling. Much later, Andrew admitted that his silence had been an aggressive act. He had seriously considered leaving the group and had wanted to prove to himself that "it was not worth a damn."

Just as the different personalities of members affect their behavior in the group, so does that of the leader. Some leaders try at first to be someone else, to adopt a style not genuinely their own. Luckily, most of them get over that rather quickly. Joe was a very effective, directive person. That was his temperament and that became his style. Bill, on the other hand, was much more relaxed and easygoing, and his leadership style mirrored this aspect of his personality. In contrast to Joe, he did not like to push or prod too hard. As he put it, he didn't look for trouble. Bob's style emphasized the consulting aspect of his role. He believed in testing out assumptions, perceptions, and behaviors, and encouraged group members to do likewise. Gloria, in the beginning, imitated her supervisor without fully realizing that she was doing so. She herself was enthusiastic and very spontaneous and found it hard to sit back for long and just listen. She enjoyed action and drama. But I will say more about this in the next chapter.

8

Training Neophyte
Group Leaders

GOALS AND METHODS

In this final chapter, I intend to deal in an organized fashion with considerations related to the training of professionals wishing to work with groups. Some of the questions that arise have been touched on in previous pages. Here, I shall try to be more specific and to present a more fully rounded picture.

The goals of such training can be formulated rather easily: to expose professionals — through methods discussed below — to the various aspects of group work, and to provide them with those learnings necessary to enable them in time to decide, hopefully in consultation with professionals more experienced than themselves, whether and to what extent group work is a field they should enter (Lakin et al., 1969). The exposure to group work must be wide and the learnings diversified. For the sake of clarity, I shall differentiate between four training stages; however, in thus differentiating, I do not wish to imply a sequential pattern. As for the time required, this is a very individual matter. My only suggestion is not to rush the process.

I begin with the **didactic** stage. Here, cognitive learnings are emphasized. These consist primarily of reading, attending lectures, discussing with others, and, most important of all, thinking. Some learn well from lectures, others learn better from books. Either means, preferably both, should provide the neophyte with a wide view of the group work area, encompassing its history, various theoretical approaches, research, and practice. The field of group dynamics should be thoroughly covered, including that of the T-Group. The relation between the young professional's earlier training and group work should be investigated. The divergent assumptions underlying the dyadic helping relationship and that of help in groups must be grasped. Journals that deal exclusively or selectively with group work should be read and kept up with.

As for books in this vast field, my modest contribution is a short but selective bibliography at the end of this text. But the field, vast as it is, is still too limited. Those who intend to work with groups should read about the human being as a social animal in literature, sociology, anthropology, history, philosophy, and religion. The list is long but is not meant to discourage. On the contrary, there is no end to fruitful and enjoyable reading for those who love people and want to understand them better.

Discussion groups, whether formal or informal, can help deal with particular topics considered in lectures and books, or they can cover a wide range of areas of interest to participants. Most of all, I recommend thinking deeply about the various aspects of group work so that, eventually, the beginner will develop a philosophy, an approach to the field. But now we are reaching the limits of the didactic stage. Beyond listening, reading, and thinking, we must begin to get the feel for what it is all about.

Working with groups is essentially a skill, and, as such, must be learned through practice. For the sake of convenience, I divide these remaining learnings into three stages, although it is evident that they are bound to overlap. The second stage, which actually should overlap with the first didactic phase, is **learning through participation.** All trainees should be members of a group at least once and preferably more than once. They must fully experience what it is like to be a group member and sample the group as a social unit in which, at first, they fulfill a limited role, that of member. Later on they will undoubtedly function as a participant observer, participating fully in the group while at the same time trying to observe all aspects of group life, concentrating especially on leader behavior. Soon they will be the authority in groups they will lead; meanwhile, they are experiencing what it feels like to cope with authority. Ideally, neophytes should be exposed to different leadership styles, but, minimally, they must participate in one group closely related to their own profession and one intensive sensitivity training workshop — this latter in order to experience group processes and to become more sensitive to their own behaviors. In addition, at some point in the training, beginners should function as nonparticipant observers. In this role they are more detached and can focus better on what is actually occurring in the group, paying closer attention to the leader's style and interventions. I shall discuss the observer's role and functions in more detail, but must state here that I consider this a very difficult part of leader training. Nevertheless, it is an essential part.

The third stage consists of **vicarious learnings,** derived particularly from filmed group sessions, partial or complete sound tapes of meetings, and written records of sessions. All of these share the advantage that they can be gone over repeatedly and discussed at leisure with peers and instructors.

In the fourth and final stage, the beginner actually begins **leading a group** — either alone or with a partner. Conjointly with this experience, the beginner should participate in more advanced seminars, and, above all, in a group of other neophytes led by a person well experienced in work with groups. To this setting, the beginner can bring doubts, hesitations, frustrations, and, last but by no means least, delight in early successes. Here the beginner can relive and restructure experiences as a leader, as well as experiment with different leader styles through role-play, role reversal, and additional techniques and exercises. Individual or group supervision or both are essential in this last training phase as the new leader approaches independence.

THE OBSERVER

In a very real sense, all group members are observers. They are participant observers. Some members are so busy participating and become so absorbed in what is taking place that they have little opportunity for observation. Others prefer to observe, and, in that role, they are both resented for their detachment and yet appealed to by other members for their perceptions of what has just occurred. Others, still, can learn to participate and observe almost simultaneously. Fred, in Gloria's group, was such a participant observer, which is why Gladys chose him to portray the role of her husband George.

Nonparticipant observers, however, only observe. They do so as part of their training, in order to promote their own learnings about groups. If their observations assist the leader and thus, indirectly, the group, so much the better, but it should be self-evident that trainees have every right to put their own learnings first.

Sid, who is in training, is ready to observe a group. His supervisor may help him to find a group to observe, or Sid may have already found one for himself. He approaches the group leader for permission to observe. If the leader agrees, but states frankly that there will not be time to meet with Sid between meetings to discuss his observations and answer questions, Sid had better find a leader with more free time. For the neophyte, observation without a mutual exchange of perceptions and explanations for the leader's specific interventions is wasteful, and may even prove harmful.

When a satisfactory arrangement has been made, leader and observer must decide whether the latter will observe within the room or from behind a one-way mirror. In either case, I believe the group should be informed and the observer role explained. Observers are not second leaders; they are not other members. They are there to observe and only to observe.

If Sid observes in the room, certain problems will arise. For instance, where should he sit? If he takes notes, he should sit apart from the group. If he does not, he may sit with the group, taking care not to sit too close to the leader. His role must define his behavior. If addressed in the group, he ought not to reply. Even when greatly tempted, he must remain silent. The leader will undoubtedly not let such provocation of the observer slip by unnoticed, but will refer it to the group for analysis, thus, incidentally, protecting Sid in his role of observer.

Observers must be left entirely free to pursue their role without having to concern themselves with possible responses to member overtures. What if observers are addressed outside of the group? There, they can be themselves, but they must still refrain from discussing group matters; of course, they may explain why. If observers should even inadvertently slip into participating, they will be changing their role. If a group agrees to allow an observer to participate, it will have gained another member, but in order to fulfill the goals of training, the neophyte will have to find another group to observe.

I know of leader-observer arrangements whereby the observer joins in the discussion when the group engages in summarizing activities. Some groups summarize at the conclusion of each session, others periodically. Such limited observer participation, if acceptable to all concerned and restricted to summation periods, can be most helpful.

Everything considered, observing is rather a thankless task for those who really wish to get moving in group work, and it should not be extended over too long a period of time. Once neophytes are ready to take on the challenge of action, they should be encouraged in that direction, unless, of course, good evidence exists for not hurrying them along. Observing is a passive, restricting, and frustrating task. It tends, over a period of time, to foster an inclination in the observer to identify with the group and resent the leader's behavior. Observers generally conclude that what the leader can do, they can do as well, if not better. Incidentally, this is an additional reason for between-session leader-observer conferences. By no means should leaders be coerced to take on observers against their inclinations, but if they do consent, this entails the responsibility of checking out group events with trainees.

CO-LEADING

As far as I am concerned, the most meaningful and rewarding training experience is co-leading. It should come toward the end of the neophyte's training program, and can be repeated from time to time thereafter to good advantage. **Co-leading** is a technique whereby two leaders work with a group at the same time. From the group's point of view, it means having to deal with and being able to learn from two leaders who participate fully in group life — not an active leader and a passive observer, nor a leader and a combination leader-member, but two full leaders.

Who co-leads with whom? For one, supervisor and trainee can co-lead, in which case their respective parts in group interaction must be clear to them both. Certain questions will arise in this situation. Does the neophyte feel free to be natural and to actually take on the leader role? To what extent does the supervisor wish to be imitated, and to what degree can the supervisor accept another's style? Does concern with grades and evaluation affect the trainee's freedom of action?

If the neophyte co-leads with an experienced leader who is not a supervisor, they must carefully consider whether they are both really willing to take on this joint enterprise. Just as some group leaders do not like to be observed, others cannot function well with another leader. Will there be sufficient time available between sessions to work on group events, leader interventions, differing perceptions, personality clashes, and possible misunderstandings? Co-leading exposes both experienced and neophyte leaders to each other's personalities, including their respective strengths and weaknesses as they appear in the group. Consequently, it cannot help being an intimate relationship; therefore, if it is to prosper, it must be based on the voluntary consent of both. Although set up to further the trainee's development, the partnership has much to offer the experienced group leader as well, for in no other situation will all of a leader's behaviors be so carefully picked up on, weighed, and submitted to discussion and feedback.

It is quite clear that at the beginning, at least, the partnership will consist of a junior and a senior partner. What strategies can they agree on before the group begins? How will the senior partner help the junior one get into the act? Will the junior get cold feet at the last moment and hold back from intervening? To what extent can they be trusting and open with each other between group sessions and, with time, within the group itself? Can they develop complementary styles of leadership, and, if not, can two very different styles be tolerated in the group? What if the partnership should fail? Will this handicap the neophyte's progress in training? Whatever the answers to these questions — and they depend primarily on the personalities of the partners — suffice it to say that an unsuccessful partnership should not be perpetuated, and certainly not at the expense of the group. But should the partners hit it off well, the co-leading experience will prove an enriching one for both.

What about the possibility of two neophytes co-leading a group? I know that this is not an unusual practice and, at times, it is even a successful one, but I still have strong reservations about it. Beginners, I believe, learn best with and from more experienced workers, those who feel secure in their role and relatively confident of their interventions. If the experienced worker is flexible, helpful, accepting of shortcomings, and ready to encourage the relative newcomer to action, the neophyte will gain a great deal from the collaboration. Two neophytes, on the other hand, may possibly reinforce each other's weaknesses, compete for power and authority, and foster each other's insecurity. They may, of course, learn from each other and not unduly harm the group in the process. I can, unfortunately, perceive other alternatives. If they are closely supervised, this is a bit more reassuring — but, frankly, not completely so.

Co-leading is not always feasible and other methods must, perforce, be accepted. I wish to mention briefly two other training procedures, which are not, by definition, co-leading. The first method consists in the neophyte functioning as sole leader. The neophyte's supervisor is present in the room, behind a one-way screen, or available for supervision immediately after the group session (which the supervisor does not observe). Had I the choice, I would not want my supervisor in the room with me as observer. If he or she were present, I would much prefer that we be co-leaders. Otherwise, whether my supervisor has observed or not, I would want the opportunity to engage in a supervisory session directly after the group meeting.

The second training procedure was developed by Jarvis and Esty (1968), who propose an alternate leader-observer technique. Here, experienced leader and neophyte function as group leader in alternate sessions. The partner not participating in the group observes from behind the one-way screen. Time is set aside for discussion after each session. Without doubt, other techniques exist and others are yet to be devised. Be that as it may, to date, I know of no substitute that even remotely approaches the benefits that can be derived from co-leading with an experienced professional group leader.

WHAT WE MUST LEARN TO ACCEPT

Group life, as we have seen, is very complex. It consists basically of three elements: the dynamics of the group, the dynamics of the personalities making up the group, and the dynamics of the leader as person and professional. To the neophytes, all of these components may seem difficult, if not impossible, to cope with at first. But learn to cope they will, with a bit of luck, much tenacity, and a real desire to succeed in group work (Yalom, 1966). I wish now to examine, or, in some instances, to re-examine, these three elements of group life. I believe that when they are divided up in this manner, they may seem less threatening, and the entire picture will therefore appear more comprehensible.

One aspect of group dynamics, which may bewilder us at first but with which we shall have to learn to live, is that of motion. Members are constantly moving in the group — now active, now passive; now tense, now relaxed; now involved, now remote; now friendly, now hostile. At times the group seems to dig deep down, trying to understand, wrestling with issues that appear to concern everyone; whereas at other times, group activity seems superficial, shallow, hardly worth pursuing. The group's mood changes — rapidly on some occasions, slowly on others. It is only when we begin to appreciate the needs of the group and the fact that these needs vary from group to group that things begin to fall into place. It took Gloria a long time to realize that her parents' group swung like a pendulum from extreme activity to unbelievable inertness. Once she adjusted herself to the rhythm of the group, she found it much easier to cope.

Some groups have a genuine need to mark time, in order to absorb what has gone before and gather energy prior to their next move. Even experienced workers cannot always know for certain whether the group is making progress or has come to a standstill. In this context, Bob did not correctly interpret the committee's behavior. He saw the standstill, but kept anticipating progress long after it should have become obvious that the committee was paralyzed. Joe, on the other hand, had little patience with groups when they marked time. He was aware that he pushed and prodded, told the group that this was the way he worked, even suggested they resist his pressure, but went on pushing and prodding just the same.

Occasionally, the leader must decide on priorities. The group as a whole should be responded to right now, but neither Dan nor Howard can be ignored. Dan's stubborn silence shouts for attention. Howard has just asked a direct question, and the group's laughter ought to be reacted to. What should come first? Will it have to be at the expense of something else? For the neophyte and the experienced leader alike these are not easy decisions to make, but experienced workers know at least that rapid decisions are required so that still more material will not pile up. They have also learned that members will frequently pick up cues a bit later and that important interactions, even if passed over for the moment, become part of a group's history and can be returned to at a later time. But most of all, they know that they are not infallible; this often helps them to make decisions.

The leader's position in the group may be confusing at times.

Leaders may shift from a central to a marginal role, or be pushed back and forth by forces beyond their control. This aspect of group dynamics puzzled Gloria greatly when she first started out. One moment all members were looking to her for the next move, and then suddenly interactions were taking place all around her, and she could not get a word in edgewise. The insight she gradually reached was that she need not immediately "rescue" the group when members seemed not to know what to do next, and — the other side of the coin — she would have to become a bit more forceful when she felt it important to make an intervention, even when group interaction was intense. As for Bill, he came to the conclusion that he did not permit himself to be central in the group, even when members needed him there for a while. With this realization, he began to shift in that direction.

The second component of the elements making up group life concerns member personalities. New leaders often fall prey to the ostensibly mild, dependent member who desires nothing more than to feed out of the leader's hand — until this member is good and ready to bite it. We may, indeed, prefer members who are independent in outlook, but shall have to learn to live with the dependent and the counterdependent as well. Ambivalent members do not make the leader's work easier either. Sometimes they are excited about the group, sometimes they dislike it; at times they demand praise and at others reject it violently. Only when we can empathize enough to feel how very hard life must be for them can we begin to accept them. Some people are attracted to groups because of a pervading sense of having been rejected. However, the moment they are approached, they reject the approacher. Once we understand the dynamics of their personality a bit better, we can help them realize just what it is that they do to others, how it feels, and how others react — in the process obligingly helping them to perpetuate the feeling of rejection. We shall, in time, become more accepting of the foibles and failings of group members — not of all, I suspect, but of most. But we can do so only under one condition: that we can accept our own foibles and failings, learning to live with them more or less comfortably.

This leads me to the third element of group life, the leader's personality. Not all leaders cope equally well with ambiguity. Bill could; Bob could to a lesser degree. The latter was ready to test things out, but he needed to know where he and others stood. Joe, as will be remembered, had no problems handling hostility, either in dishing it out or taking it. He experienced far more trouble, however, with the expression of warmth, friendliness, and intimacy. With Gloria it was just the other way around. She knew she needed to be liked and truly liked others. When group members expressed feelings of tenderness and love, she felt warm and happy, but when people shouted or attacked each other, Gloria trembled within. With the passage of time, she became more resilient. Essentially, of course, she remained the same Gloria.

TRAINING NEEDS AND PERSONAL NEEDS

And now it is time to bring things to a close. I shall end this book as I began it: with the personal needs of the neophyte group leader — but here I shall remain within the framework of training. If the training you are undergoing does not answer your personal needs, by all means try to obtain it elsewhere, but first check carefully whether group work is really for you. Not everyone is suited to lead groups. Not everyone functions best or even adequately in the leader role. People can be helped in many diverse ways; it need not necessarily be done in groups. Your participation in a qualified training program over a reasonable period of time should provide an indication, at least, of whether you are headed in the right direction. But the best guide of all is your own inner voice. It will tell you if group work is the area in which you can perform well and, at the same time, find satisfaction. Listen to it.

If you cannot learn to overcome your fear of the group, or, at least, to cope with it sufficiently so that it does not hamper your work or embitter your personal life, you should not persist too long. Most beginners are uncertain, anxious, and fearful, but if the passage of time and further experience do not bolster your self-confidence, group work is most likely not for you.

If, on the other hand, your training is proceeding satisfactorily — with, of course, unavoidable ups and downs — it will become essential for you to discover your own style of leading, not that of your supervisor or of your co-leader, but your own personal style. As you gradually become aware of it, you will be able to test it out and mold it to your particular needs and preferences. This is not only a legitimate process, but it is important for your development as an independent, professional group leader.

In Parting

When the group reaches its last session and is about to terminate, it is often difficult to break away and leave. Feelings previously expressed are expressed once more. Thoughts stated are stated again. Parting words already spoken are repeated. Nothing new can be explored, nothing more be added. And yet everyone stands around, reluctant to leave — one more glance, another handclasp and pat on the back, another hug and kiss. With me, it is something like that right now. I really have nothing more to add, but I am finding it hard to leave. So, just a few more words and I shall be on my way.

I hope you will enjoy your group — even the first one for which you alone will be responsible. If you can enjoy it despite the confusion, the frustration, and the uncertainty, you will know that you are on the right road. I don't know how you will feel, but I, personally, enjoy the excitement, the tension, the working together, the gradual formation of a new social unit in which everyone finds his or her place. I enjoy watching people getting to know each other and getting to know themselves better — and I like being part of it. I enjoy being with people who try to grow and change, and, most of all I think, I like to see people helping one another and to feel myself involved in the process.

I enjoy working with just one other person in a dyadic relationship, too. But that is different. It is not better or worse, but it is not the same. When we are only two, we can concentrate fully on one another and delve deeply into the client's inner world. But sometimes I wish we had a group there to help us, to give us feedback. In the group, it's just the other way around. There I often wish I were alone with just that member who is speaking now; examining, exploring, discovering — soon to be interrupted by group interests or the claims of other individuals. What I mean, I suppose, is that I enjoy both the group and the dyad, and hope you will enjoy them both as well, the one reinforcing the other.

I really am going now, but first want to point out that I have omitted much from this text. I have not mentioned work with couples or families or children or . . . and I won't begin now.

I know, we have to be on our way. Don't forget: you learn most by doing. Progress in stages. Get all the support you can. Discover your own unique style. Do not give up too easily. Playing duets is fun; so is leading a small orchestra. Enjoy your group!

A Selected Bibliography

Articles recommended for the neophyte

Adams, H. J., and Barr, D. J. "A Model for Training Group Counselors." *Counselor Education and Supervision* 11(1) (1971): 36–40.

Betz, R. L. "Effects of Group Counseling as an Adjunctive Practicum Experience." *Journal of Counseling Psychology* 16(6) (1969): 528–533.

Dyer, W. G. "An Inventory of Trainer Interventions." In *Group Procedures: Purposes, Processes and Outcomes*, edited by R. C. Diedrich and H. A. Dye, pp. 115–119. Boston: Houghton Mifflin, 1972.

* Gibb, J. R. "Defensive Communication." *Journal of Communication* 11(3) (1961): 141–148.

* Jarvis, P. E., and Esty, J. F. "The Alternate-Therapist-Observer Technique in Group Therapy Training." *International Journal of Group Psychotherapy* 18(1) (1968): 95–99.

*† Lakin, M.; Lieberman, M. A.; and Whitaker, D. S. "Issues in the Training of Group Psychotherapists." *International Journal of Group Psychotherapy* 19(3) (1969): 307–325.

Levin, S., and Kanter, S. S. "Some General Considerations in the Supervision of Beginning Group Psychotherapists." *International Journal of Group Psychotherapy* 14(3) (1964): 318–331.

Orton, J. W. "Areas of Focus in Supervising Counseling Practicum Students in Groups." *Personnel and Guidance Journal* 44(2) (1965): 167–170.

Sollinger, I.; Yarosy, E.; Loughram, G.; and Sebald, D. "Training for Group Work." *Journal of Employment Counseling* 8(1) (1971): 19–25.

---

* Referred to in the text.
† Especially recommended for the neophyte.

Tate, T. E. "Counseling Groups for Counselor Trainees: A Process Model." *Counselor Education and Supervision* 13(1) (1973): 68–72.

Williams, M. "Limitations, Fantasies and Security Operations of Beginning Group Psychotherapists." *International Journal of Group Psychotherapy* 16(2) (1966): 150–162.

*† Yalom, I. D. "Problems of Neophyte Group Therapists." *International Journal of Social Psychiatry* 12(1) (1966): 52–59.

Books recommended for the neophyte

GROUP COUNSELING

Button, L. *Development Group Work with Adolescents*. London: University of London Press, 1974.

† Dinkmeyer, D. C., and Muro, J. J. *Group Counseling: Theory and Practice*. Itasca, Ill.: F. E. Peacock, 1971.

Fullmer, D. W. *Counseling: Group Theory and System*. Toronto: International Textbook Co., 1971.

† Gazda, G. M. *Group Counseling*. Boston: Allyn & Bacon, 1971.

† Gazda, G. M., ed. *Theories and Methods of Group Counseling in the Schools*. Springfield, Ill.: Thomas, 1972.

Glanz, E. C., and Hayes, R. W. *Groups in Guidance*. 2nd ed. Boston: Allyn & Bacon, 1967.

Kemp, C. G. *Foundations of Group Counseling*. New York: McGraw-Hill, 1970.

Macleman, B. W., and Felsenfeld, N. *Group Counseling and Psychotherapy with Adolescents*. New York: Columbia University Press, 1968.

† Ohlsen, M. M. *Group Counseling*. New York: Holt, Rinehart & Winston, 1970.

Slavson, S. R. *Child-Centered Group Guidance of Parents*. New York: International University Press, 1958.

GROUP DYNAMICS AND GROUP WORK

Auerbach, A. S. *Parents Learn Through Discussion: Principles and Practices of Parent Group Education*. New York: John Wiley, 1968.

* Bales, R. F. *Personality and Interpersonal Behavior*. New York: Holt, Rinehart & Winston, 1970.

* Bales, R. F.; Hare, A. P.; and Borgatta, E. F. *Small Groups, Studies in Social Interaction*. New York: Knopf, 1965.

Batten, T. R. *The Non-Directive Approach in Group and Community Work*. London: Oxford University Press, 1967.

Button, L. *Discovery and Experience: A New Approach to Training, Group Work and Teaching*. London: Oxford University Press, 1971.

Diedrich, R. C., and Dye, A. H., eds. *Group Procedures, Purposes, Processes and Outcomes*. Boston: Houghton Mifflin, 1972.

Driver, H. I., et al. *Counseling and Learning Through Small Group Discussion*. Madison, Wis.: Monona Publications, 1962.

Dyer, W. G., ed. *Modern Theory and Method in Group Training*. New York: Van Nostrand Reinhold, 1972.

Kaye, B., and Rogers, I. *Group Work in Secondary Schools and the Training of Teachers in its Methods*. London: Oxford University Press, 1968.

Kemp, C. G. *Perspectives on the Group Process*. Boston: Houghton Mifflin, 1970.

Knowles, M., and Knowles, H. *Introduction to Group Dynamics*. Rev. ed. New York: Association Press, 1972.

† Lifton, W. M. *Groups: Facilitating Individual Growth and Societal Change*. New York: John Wiley, 1972.

* Luft, J. *Group Processes*. 2nd ed. Palo Alto, Cal.: National Press, 1970.

Miles, M. *Learning to Work in Groups*. New York: Columbia University Press, 1967.

Mills, T. M. *The Sociology of Small Groups*. Englewood Cliffs, N.J.: Prentice-Hall, 1967.

† Napier, R., and Gershenfeld, M. K. *Groups: Theory and Experience*. Boston: Houghton Mifflin, 1973.

Newman, R. G. *Groups in Schools*. New York: Simon & Schuster, 1974.

Olmsted, M. *The Small Group*. New York: Random House, 1966.

Patton, B., and Giffin, K. *Problem-Solving Group Interaction*. New York: Harper & Row, 1973.

Patton, B., and Giffin, K., eds. *Interpersonal Communication*. New York: Harper & Row, 1974.

Schmuck, R. A., and Schmuck, P. A. *Group Processes in the Classroom*. 2nd ed. Dubuque, Iowa: Brown, 1975.

Shaw, M. *Group Dynamics: The Psychology of Small Group Behavior*. New York: McGraw-Hill, 1971.

Slater, P. *Microcosm*. New York: John Wiley, 1966.

Thelen, H. A. *Dynamics of Groups at Work*. Chicago: University of Chicago Press, 1970.

Thompson, S., and Katz, H. *The Group Process as a Helping Technique*. Oxford: Pergamon Press, 1973.

GROUP PSYCHOTHERAPY

Appley, D. G., and Winder, A. E. *T-Groups and Therapy Groups in a Changing Society*. San Francisco: Jossey-Bass, 1973.

Bach, G. R. *Intensive Group Psychotherapy*. New York: Ronald Press, 1954.

* Bion, W. R. *Experiences in Groups and Other Papers*. London: Tavistock, 1961.

Durkin, H. E. *The Group in Depth*. New York: International University Press, 1968.

Foulkes, S. H., and Anthony, E. J. *Group Psychotherapy: The Psychoanalytic Approach*. London: Penguin Books, 1965.

Gazda, G. M. *Basic Approach to Group Psychotherapy and Group Counseling*. Springfield, Ill.: Thomas, 1970.

Gazda, G. M., ed. *Innovations to Group Psychotherapy*, Springfield, Ill.: Thomas, 1970.

Ginott, H. G. *Group Psychotherapy with Children*. New York: McGraw-Hill, 1961.

Johnson, J. A. *Group Therapy: A Practical Approach*. New York: McGraw-Hill, 1963.

Kadis, A. L., and Krausner, J. O. *A Practicum of Group Psychotherapy*. New York: Harper & Row, 1970.

Kaplan, H. I., and Sadock, B. J., eds. *Comprehensive Group Psychotherapy*. Baltimore: Williams & Wilkins, 1971.

Klapman, J. W. *Group Psychotherapy: Theory and Practice*. 2nd ed. New York: Grune & Stratton, 1959.

Maré, P. B. de, and Kreeger, L. C. *Introduction to Group Treatment in Psychiatry*. London: Butterworths, 1974.

Mowrer, O. H. *The New Group Therapy*. New York: Van Nostrand, 1964.

Mullan, H., and Rosenbaum, M. *Group Psychotherapy: Theory and Practice*. New York: Free Press of Glencoe, 1963.

Pinney, E. *A First Group Psychotherapy Book*. Springfield, Ill.: C. Thomas, 1970.

Powdermaker, F. B., and Frank, J. D. *Group Psychotherapy Studies in Methodology of Research and Therapy*. Westport, Conn.: Greenwood Press, 1972.

Rose, S. O. *Treating Children in Groups: A Behavioral Approach*. San Francisco: Jossey-Bass, 1974.

Sager, C. J., and Kaplan, H. S., eds. *Progress in Group and Family Therapy*. New York: Brunner Mazel, 1972.

Schiffer, M. *The Therapeutic Play Group*. London: Allen & Unwin, 1971.

Slavson, S. R., ed. *Analytic Group Psychotherapy with Children, Adolescents and Adults*. New York: Columbia University Press, 1962.

Slavson, S. R. *An Introduction to Group Therapy*. New York: International University Press, 1973.

Whitaker, D. S., and Lieberman, M. A. *Psychotherapy Through the Group Process*. London: Tavistock, 1965.

*† Yalom, I. D. *Theory and Practice of Group Psychotherapy*. 2nd ed. New York: Basic Books, 1975.

SOCIAL GROUP WORK

Glasser, P., et al., eds. *Individual Change Through Small Groups*. New York: The Free Press, 1974.

Hartford, M. E. *Groups in Social Work*. New York: Columbia University Press, 1972.

† Konopka, G., ed. *Social Group Work: A Helping Process*. Englewood Cliffs, N.J.: Prentice-Hall, 1972.

McCullough, M. K., and Ely, P. J. *Social Work with Groups*. London: Routledge & Kegan Paul, 1968.

Northen, H. *Social Work with Groups*. New York: Columbia University Press, 1969.

Schwartz, W., and Serapio, Z. R., eds. *The Practice of Group Work*. New York: Columbia University Press, 1971.

Trecker, H. B. *Social Group Work: Principles and Practices*. New York: Association Press, 1972.

T-GROUPS AND SENSITIVITY TRAINING

Back, K. W. *Beyond Words: The Story of Sensitivity Training and the Encounter Movement.* New York: Russell Sage Foundation, 1972.

* Benjamin, A. *Sensitivity Training Workshop for Arab and Jewish Students.* Translated from the Hebrew. Jerusalem, Israel: The American Jewish Committee, 1972.

Benne, K. D., et al. *The Laboratory Method of Changing and Learning — Theory and Application.* Palo Alto: Science and Behavior Books, Inc., 1975.

Berger, M. L., and Berger, J. *Group Training Techniques.* New York: John Wiley, 1972.

Blank, L., et al., eds. *Confrontation: Encounters in Self- and Interpersonal Awareness.* New York: Macmillan, 1971.

* Bradford, L. P., et al., eds. *T-Group Therapy and Laboratory Method: Innovation in Re-Education.* New York: John Wiley, 1965.

Burton, A., ed. *Encounter.* San Francisco: Jossey-Bass, 1969.

Egan, G. *Face to Face: The Small Group, Experience and Interpersonal Growth.* Monterey, Calif.: Brooks Cole, 1973.

* Golembiewski, R. T., and Blumberg, A., eds. *Sensitivity Training and the Laboratory Approach.* 2nd ed. Itasca, Ill.: F. E. Peacock, 1970, 1973.

Howard, J. *Please Touch: A Guided Tour of the Human Potential Movement.* New York: McGraw-Hill, 1970.

*† Lakin, M. *Interpersonal Encounter: Theory and Practice in Sensitivity Training.* New York: McGraw-Hill, 1972.

* Lieberman, M. A., et al. *Encounter Groups: First Facts.* New York: Basic Books, 1973.

Malamud, D. I., and Machover, S. *Toward Self Understanding: Group Techniques in Self Confrontation.* Springfield, Ill.: C. Thomas, 1970.

Mintz, E. E. *Marathon Groups: Symbol and Reality.* New York: Appleton-Century-Crofts, 1971.

Ottaway, A. K. *Learning Through Group Experience.* London: Routledge & Kegan Paul, 1968.

Rice, A. *Learning for Leadership.* London: Tavistock, 1965.

Rogers, C. R. *On Encounter Groups.* New York: Harper & Row, 1970.

Ruitenbeek, H. M. *The New Group Therapies.* New York: Discus, 1970.

Schaffer, J. B., and Galinsky, D. M. *Models of Group Therapy and Sensitivity Training.* Englewood Cliffs, N.J.: Prentice-Hall, 1974.

* Schein, E. H., and Bennis, W. G. *Personal and Organizational Change Through Group Methods: The Laboratory Approach.* New York: John Wiley, 1967.

Schutz, W. C. *Joy: Expanding Human Awareness.* New York: Grove, 1968.

Smith, H. C. *Sensitivity Training: The Scientific Understanding of Individuals.* New York: McGraw-Hill, 1973.

Solomon, L. and Berzon, B., eds. *New Perspectives on Encounter Groups.* San Francisco: Jossey-Bass, 1972.

MISCELLANEOUS RECOMMENDED BOOKS

Barker, L. *Listening Behavior.* Englewood Cliffs, N.J.: Prentice-Hall, 1971.

* Benjamin, A. *The Helping Interview.* 2nd ed. Boston: Houghton Mifflin, 1974.

Bergin, A., and Garfield, S. *Handbook of Psychotherapy and Behavior Change.* New York: John Wiley, 1971.

* Bugental, J. F. *The Search for Authenticity.* New York: Holt, Rinehart & Winston, 1965.

* Carkhuff, R. R. *The Development of Human Resources.* New York: Holt, Rinehart & Winston, 1971.

Fagan, J., and Shepard, I., eds. *Gestalt Therapy Now.* Cupertino, Calif.: Science and Behavior Books, 1970.

* Frank, J. D. *Persuasion and Healing.* New York: Schocken, 1961.

Freud, S. *Group Psychology and the Analysis of the Ego.* Complete Works, vol. XVII. London: Hogarth, 1955.

Golembiewski, R. T. *Renewing Organizations.* Itasca, Ill.: F. E. Peacock, 1972.

Harris, T. *I'm O.K. — You're O.K.* New York: Harper & Row, 1969.

* Lindzey, G., and Byrne, D. "Measurement of Social Choice and

Interpersonal Attractiveness." In *The Handbook of Social Psychology*, edited by G. Lindzey and E. Aronson. Vol. 2. 2nd ed. Reading, Mass.: Addison Wesley, 1969.

* Maier, N. R. F., et al. *Supervisory and Executive Development: A Manual for Role Playing.* New York: John Wiley, 1967.

* Middleman, R. R. *The Non-Verbal in Working with Groups.* New York. Association Press, 1970.

*† Moreno, J. L. *Who Shall Survive? Foundations of Sociometry, Group Psychotherapy and Sociodrama.* Rev. ed. New York: Beacon House, 1953.

* Northway, M. L. *A Primer of Sociometry.* Toronto: University of Toronto Press, 1967.

* Perls, F. S. *Gestalt Therapy Verbatim.* San Francisco: Real People Press, 1969.

White, R. K., and Lippitt, R. *Autocracy and Democracy.* New York: Harper & Row, 1960.

Index